BEDSIDE BOOK OF
BAD GIRLS

OUTLAW WOMEN OF THE MIDWEST

BY CHRIS ENSS

FARCOUNTRY
PRESS

HELENA, MONTANA

ISBN 10: 1-56037-525-6
ISBN 13: 978-1-56037-525-8

© 2012 by Farcountry Press
Text © 2012 by Chris Enss

Cover photo: Left: "Victoria Hull." Special Collections, Vassar College Libraries; Center: "Poker Alice of
Sturgis." Photo Courtesy of the State Archives of the South Dakota Historical Society; Right: "Kate King."
Jackson County (Mo.) Historical Society Archives.
Back cover photo: istockphoto.com

For more information on our books, write Farcountry Press, P.O. Box 5630, Helena, MT 59604;
call (800) 821-3874; or visit www.farcountrypress.com.

Library of Congress Cataloging-in-Publication Data

Enss, Chris, 1961-
   Bedside book of bad girls : outlaw women of the Midwest / by Chris Enss.
      p. cm.
   Includes bibliographical references and index.
   ISBN 978-1-56037-525-8
1. Women outlaws--Middle West--Case studies. 2. Crime--Middle West--History--19th century. 3. Middle
West--History--19th century. I. Title.
   HV6452.M555E53 2012
   364.1092'520977--dc23
                                    2012013115

Created, produced, and designed in the United States.
Printed in United States.

17   16   15   14   13   12   1   2   3   4   5   6   .

TABLE OF CONTENTS

ACKNOWLEDGMENTS

I can only try to thank all those who helped with this book.

First let me express my gratitude to Jeff Galpin, a gentleman graphic artist who went out of his way to help secure the artwork needed for several chapters in this book.

I'm indebted to Lauren Leeman at the State Historical Society of Missouri; Paul Ford at *Harper's Weekly* archives; David Jackson, director of Archives and Education at the Jackson County Historical Society in Missouri; Nancy Sherbert in the Archives Department at the Kansas State Historical Society; Dean Rogers, Special Collections Assistant at Vassar College Library; the staff at the Madelyn Helling Library in Nevada City, California; and finally to Roger Creed in Palestine, Illinois.

From Denver, Colorado, to Independence, Missouri, so many knowledgeable people offered their expertise—assisting during my onsite research. They provided valuable historical documents to use in writing this book, and generously offered to help in tracking down hard-to-find information. To all I humbly say, "Thank you."

INTRODUCTION

his edition of the *Bedside Book of Bad Girls* chronicles 110 years of Midwestern banditry. This lawlessness was spawned in part by the Civil War and finally checked by the Federal Bureau of Investigation. Some outlaws, such as Frank and Jesse James and the Younger Brothers, blamed the oppressive troops of the Union Army as a reason for their wrongdoings. They claimed that Southern sympathizers were treated poorly after the war and denied the chance to earn an honest living. Ma Barker and her boys felt similarly afflicted by the federal government. They insisted that they were unable to secure legitimate work because authorities were always accusing them of major crimes.

A shocking array of high crimes and misdemeanors committed in such places as North Platte, Nebraska; Lawrence, Illinois; Labette County, Kansas; and Joplin, Missouri; were perpetrated by women. Whether wicked by nature or choice, the renegade women profiled in this book—and those whose names have been lost to history—resisted living law-abiding lives. Tales of history's bad girls and outlaw women are not as well publicized as those of Joaquin Murrieta, John Wesley Hardin, the James Brothers, Benjamin "Bugsy" Siegel, and Meyer Lansky, but they are no less stirring, and their illegal exploits are as riveting as anything their male counterparts carried out.

The American Midwest was a place of great opportunity during the nineteenth century, teeming with explorers, farmers, missionaries, trappers, and traders, all striving to carve out a living for themselves. Homesteaders, ranchers, shop owners, and railroad executives established towns and cities that dared to reach beyond the boundaries of the Mississippi River toward the Pacific Ocean. Outlaws stalked the region as well, taking advantage of cowboys coming off the trail; immigrants passing through on stagecoaches, wagons, or trains; and disenfranchised Native Americans trying to hold on to their land.

By the mid-1930s, the American Midwest had progressed substantially. Automobiles replaced Conestoga wagons, and the sod houses pioneers called home were replaced with brick and mortar. Ambitious settlers had transformed small communities like Minneapolis, Minnesota; St. Louis, Missouri; and Chicago, Illinois; into bustling metropolises. Hardships, however, came with the advancements. A devastating drought brought the Dust Bowl, and a severe economic downturn thrust the country into the Great Depression. Outlaws again took advantage of the desperate times.

Among the notorious bad guys who robbed, swindled, and murdered Midwesterners from 1824 to 1936 were a number of bad girls who could be just as dishonest and violent. Female fugitives such as Flora Mundis, a horse thief and prostitute, were motivated by poverty, lack of opportunity, discontent, and a desire for adventure. Others, such as serial killer Kate Bender, were driven by a cold-blooded, cruel character that made them ruthless and inhumane. Some, such as Sarah Quantrill, became wanted women by association; these ladies harbored their outlaw lovers and aided them in their criminal behavior.

Just as male outlaws experienced retribution from the long arm of the law, female criminals paid a price as well. Federal agents and local authorities tracked lady desperados to their hideouts and arrested them. Some received fair trials and served time or were executed. Others were killed on the spot for their misdeeds.

In writing the stories of these lawless females for this book, every attempt was made to separate legend from truth. Newspaper accounts and oral interpretation of events passed down from generation to generation make that mission impossible at times. Women outlaws were intriguing to dime novelists and reporters, and their exploits were often exaggerated to make the women and their crimes more sensational.

In addition to sifting through actual events and outlandish claims, historians write from the dim distance of decades. Dates and broad particulars can be argued. What is not debatable is that these women contributed to the criminal history of the dashing days of the wild and woolly Midwest. ✺

CHAPTER ONE

FLORA MUNDIS
Lady Horse Thief

Tom King followed five spirited, fast-moving horses into a dense line of trees seven miles outside the town of Fredonia, Kansas. It was a stifling hot August day in 1894. Low-hanging branches on brown, thirsty trees slapped at the criminal and his horse as they sped by. Sweat foamed around the animal's neck and hindquarters. Tom, dressed in worn trousers, chaps, a flannel shirt, a large-brimmed hat, and a tan duster, skillfully maneuvered his ride around fallen limbs in pursuit of his quarry.

Tom and his roan were directly beside the five horses as they broke through the other side of the grove of trees. His horse leapt over a cluster of large boulders; Tom leaned back in the saddle to let the wind strip off his coat as his horse jumped. In that moment Tom and the horse were in midair, and the coat trailed behind him like leather wings.

From a crude camp far in the distance, Fredonia Sheriff H. S. Mc-Cleary watched Tom and his mount keep pace with the horses. The lawman cast a glance at the deputies standing on either side of him. Their eyes were fixed on Tom. If not for the fact that the authorities were there to arrest Tom for stealing horses, they might have felt compelled to congratulate him on his equestrian skills. They had apprehended Tom's partner, Ed Bullock, at the thieves' camp, placed a gag around his mouth, and handcuffed him to the back of a wagon. Beside the wagon was a large trunk filled with an assortment of stolen jewelry.

Bullock tugged at the handcuffs in a desperate attempt to break free. He wanted, somehow, to warn Tom not to return to camp. It was too late. Tom led the ill-gotten horses into the camp, and right into the arms of the law. The sheriff leveled his gun at the bandit, and Tom slowly dismounted. He surrendered his weapon without having to be asked. The sheriff took a few steps toward Tom, studying his face as he walked. According to the *San Antonio Daily Light* on August 16, 1894, the sun and wind had darkened King's complexion, and at first glance he appeared to be a mixed-blood Cherokee Indian. Sheriff McCleary asked him how old he was, and Tom told him his age was twenty-five. The sheriff scrutinized Tom's face, then told him to remove his hat. In that moment it was clear that the notorious Tom King was no man at all. The outlaw that stood before him was a woman named Flora Mundis.

Ed Bullock wasn't a man either. She was Jesse Whitewings. Both women were from the Cottonwood Creek bottoms of West Guthrie, Oklahoma. Flora had been arrested twice in the last two years but managed to escape before standing trial for her crimes. Knowing Flora's history, Sheriff McCleary wasted no time taking the two women to his jail in Canadian County. He would not make the same mistake other lawmen had who were too intimidated by the fact that the wanted horse thieves were indeed ladies; he was determined to treat them like the criminals they were.

On August 17, 1894, the *El Reno Democrat* reported that once the women were locked up, the sheriff recognized how difficult it would be for his deputies to follow his example. "There is something ominous to the atmosphere of the jail here . . . a death-like quietude and a tip-toe carefulness about the place not common of men used to handling hardened criminals. The officials appear awkward and confused, and the turnkey is beside himself. The famous woman, who has caused so much trouble in the past, is going to cause much more in the immediate future. The jailers have arranged it so that a physician is near at hand . . . although some believe the event will take place without accident."

Flora Mundis was born Flora Quick in Johnson County, Missouri, in 1875. Her father, Daniel Quick, was a wealthy rancher and farmer. He was married twice and fathered fifteen children. Flora was the youngest daughter and his favorite child. She possessed considerable talent, and at fourteen Daniel enrolled her at Holden College, a school for the arts in Holden, Missouri. In less than a month, Flora left school and returned home. She didn't like being confined to a classroom and preferred instead to ride her horse around the family estate.

Flora's father died in 1890. The twenty-four acres of land he owned, as well as 13,000 dollars in personal property, were divided equally among his children. Flora's oldest brother was named executor of their father's holdings, and, in addition to taking charge of the finances, he assumed responsibility for his siblings. He decided to send his headstrong sister Flora to a school in nearby Sedalia. He hoped that while there she would settle down and marry a man of good, moral character. Flora did the exact opposite.

After a brief stay in school, she dropped out and married an older, disreputable man named Ora Mundis. Family and friends warned Flora that he was untrustworthy and only after her share of her father's estate. She didn't believe them. She thought Ora was exciting. The couple spent their evenings in Holden visiting the saloons along the main thoroughfare of town, drinking and gambling. Quickly bored with the nightly routine, the newlyweds decided to take off on a hunting expedition. The Mundises returned to Holden one year later. They boasted to anyone they met about their encounters with the law and how the Indian Nation (the Pawnee, Osage, Kiowa, and Arapaho) feared them. They warned Holden residents that they were "bad, bad people that were not to be trifled with." Holden's city marshal was not intimidated by the pair. He relieved them of their guns and strongly suggested they leave town.

Shortly after Flora sold her share of the family estate, she and her husband left Holden and headed for Guthrie. They arrived at the growing Oklahoma rail town in November 1892. Flora was seventeen years old and Ora was thirty.

The two lived a fast lifestyle, gambling, drinking, purchasing fine clothing and fine horses, until Flora's money ran out. Ora left her soon after that. Desperate and penniless, Flora turned to prostitution. During the day she

After her husband's departure, Flora turned to prostitution to make ends meet. Often she was seen riding through town in one of her iconic equestrian costumes. In addition to using prostitution as a means for money, Flora also traded her services for horses and places to keep livestock she had stolen along with her friend and madam, Jesse Whitewings. ©1978 UNIVERSITY OF OKLAHOMA PRESS

could often be seen riding her horse through town dressed in an equestrian costume she had purchased with her inheritance. According to the September 26, 1893, edition of the *Cedar Rapids Evening Gazette*, she dressed in green and black gowns and "wore upon her head a black turban trimmed with a gold braid, which glistened brightly in the sun or under the electric lights." A curious reporter for the *Guthrie Daily Leader* sat down with Flora at the saloon where she worked and dared to ask her what had become of her husband. "I don't know," she told him. "We didn't get along well and fought everyday. I suspect he's better company now," she offered solemnly.

During Flora's time in Guthrie, she became good friends with a madam and gambler named Jesse Whitewings, and the pair began to steal horses. When they weren't stealing, they were trading their services for horses or money to acquire a place to keep their stolen livestock.

Flora's first tussle with the law did not involve stolen horses or prostitution but a claim of assault she made against a prominent physician in the area. Frustrated that he spurned her advances, Flora falsely charged Dr. Jordan with attacking and trying to rape her. Convinced a jury would believe the teary-eyed, tawny beauty, Dr. Jordan decided to flee the territory rather than go to court. The allegation backfired, causing irreparable harm to Flora's business. Clients stopped visiting her because they feared similar accusations. Faced with being a pauper, Flora decided to pursue stealing horses full time. She traded in her fancy clothes for cowboy gear and set off to solidify her position in outlaw history.

During the spring of 1893, she brazenly stole numerous horses from hitching posts outside stores, and from family farms and ranches. She then took the stolen animals to her hideout in an area called Hell's Fringe. Any animal that was carrying a brand was quickly re-branded and sold. Two well-known lawmen from Oklahoma City named Chris Madsen and Heck Thomas tracked a few hundred stolen animals to the outlaw's hideout in Canadian County, and Flora was subsequently arrested. Given her rough, dusty appearance and the men's clothing she was wearing, the lawmen did not suspect she was a woman. When she was apprehended, she told them her name was Tom King.

In June 1893, Tom King was thrown in jail alongside Ernest Lewis. Lewis, nicknamed "the Killer," was incarcerated for murder and suspicion of robbing a train. Tom and Ernest became fast friends, and Ernest convinced the horse thief that train robbery was the better venture. Tom agreed to help his new partner escape the Oklahoma City jail and start formulating a plan to hold up a train.

On June 27, 1893, Tom revealed her true self to an impressionable guard. She seduced him and locked him in her cell. Tom then let Ernest out of his cell, and the two fled on a pair of stolen horses. The criminals made their way to a place called the Outlet (a sixty-eight-mile-wide strip of land south of the Oklahoma/Kansas border) and immediately set their sights on robbing the Santa Fe Railway train. Tom hired a friend named Manvel to help them get the job done. At 3:30 P.M. on June 29, 1893, the trio went into action.

Carrying a rifle in his coat, Manvel boarded the train in Oklahoma City and hid himself in the smoking car. When the train reached Black Bear Creek between Red Rock and Wharton, Manvel was supposed to overpower the conductor and order him to stop the train. Tom and Ernest were waiting there to board the locomotive and rob it. The conductor, however, did not

Flora Quick Mundis effectively disguised herself as a man and took the name Tom King. This drawing from the Oswego Daily Times, *dated September 14, 1893, depicts the notorious horse thief when she was captured.* OSWEGO DAILY TIMES

let the outlaw get the upper hand. He wrested Manvel's gun from him, knocking him out in the process. Manvel was arrested—but not before divulging the whereabouts of Tom and Ernest.

When the train didn't stop, Tom and Ernest realized something had gone wrong. They decided to separate and leave the area before law enforcement arrived. Ernest headed to Colorado and Tom remained in Oklahoma. One attempt at train robbery seemed enough; she returned to stealing horses.

Authorities searched the Oklahoma Territory looking for Tom King. On July 12, 1893, Deputy Robacker of Guthrie spotted the wanted horse thief at a livery stable in town. She was sitting atop her ride talking with a few men, completely unaware she had been recognized by the law. She was arrested and returned to the same Oklahoma jail from which she had escaped only two weeks before.

By August 8, 1893, Tom had broken out of jail again and fled to a town twenty miles west of Oklahoma City called Yukon. As reported by the *Cedar Rapids Evening Gazette* on September 26, 1893, "the chase after King was marked by two incidents, one tragic and the other sensational. In the darkness two parties of searchers mistook each other for horse thieves and opened fire with Winchesters," the article read. "Will Fightmaster, son of the sheriff, was killed. Another party of deputies discovered a young woman in male attire in company with a young man in a secluded spot in the woods. They thought of course they had caught Tom King but this young woman turned out to be a well-known railroad man's wife out for a lark."

Tom was recaptured and hauled back to Oklahoma City. This time the jailer locked her in a steel cage. Her stay at the facility was brief, however. Law enforcement agents in Canadian County demanded the outlaw be turned over to them to be tried for horse theft.

Deputy Marshals Chris Madsen and Heck Thomas loaded Tom and several other prisoners onto a wagon and transported them across Oklahoma to El Reno, another town in the central portion of the territory. The crafty horse thief managed to break out of that jail, too, on December 5, 1893. The headline across the top of the December 8, 1893, *Cedar Rapids Evening Gazette* read, "Tom King, the Romantic Horse Thief, Breaks El Reno Jail in her Third Escape; She is Bound to Make a Record!" The article read:

It seems there is no jail that can hold her. Even the Oklahoma City jail, which is considered the strongest in the Territory, yielded before her magic art. . . . She is very cunning and clever. The vigilant officers usually get her, but getting her does not seem to be of much effect in curing the mania with which she is afflicted. She finds the same delight in horse stealing as other women would in reading novels or playing croquet. It is her ambition to be the most famous horse thief of her generation, and already she has taken more of them than any man in the history of the Southwest.

Included in the search team to recapture Tom in the winter of 1893 was a pack of bloodhounds. Tom managed to elude all but one of the dogs. He followed her across southern Canadian and Wichita Counties to a point near the Kiowa-Comanche-Apache reservation line. At some point Tom was able to subdue the animal and prevent it from coming after her again. On December 17, 1893, the *Guthrie Daily Leader* reported that the hound had been shot at close range. "He evidently had caught her trouser leg," the article explained, "for beside where the dog lay was a piece of Scotch-Tweed of irregular form and about the size of the sole of a man's shoe, which is said to be a piece of the suit of men's clothes which Missus King was allowed to wear in jail."

Between January and August 1894 Tom kept a very low profile. Rumors that she had formed her own gang and was crisscrossing Oklahoma carrying out various crimes circulated among law enforcement officers in Guthrie and Oklahoma City. One of the men suspected of partnering with Tom in a series of horse thefts around Tecumseh, Oklahoma, was Bill Dalton. Bill was a bank robber and the brother of Gratton, Bob, and Emmett of the famous Dalton Gang.

According to the *San Antonio Daily Light* on August 16, 1894, Bill Dalton participated in a poker game in which he put up Tom's prized horse as a bet. The incident reportedly went as follows: "Flora Mundis, alias Tom King's career as a horse thief ended with her arrest on August 7, 1894 in Fredonia, Kansas. She was extradited to Canadian County, Oklahoma, and a trial was set. She was visibly pregnant when she went before the judge and although convicted of stealing horses he did not sentence her to serve any time in jail. King was released on bail and left the Territory."

Oklahoma lawman Heck Thomas believed King was killed in an attempted bank robbery in southern Arizona. Thomas told a reporter for the *Guthrie Daily Leader* that the description and measurements of the outlaw shot at the scene of the crime matched those of the infamous King.

The last anyone heard from Tom King was late April 1896. Oklahoma City attorney D. C. Lewis, one of King's friends, received a letter from her that stated she was headed West by train. She promised to visit Lewis around Christmas but never showed. What really happened to Tom King and her child is a mystery. ⊶

CHAPTER TWO

ELIZABETH REED

The Poisonous Lady

A violent commotion inside a dilapidated cabin on the Embarras River near Lawrenceville, Illinois, broke the silence of the forest. A clay pitcher crashed through a dirty window, and the sound of two people arguing echoed across the ancient grove of pine and fir trees surrounding the crude dwelling.

It was late December 1824, and Elizabeth Fail, a painfully thin fifteen-year-old girl, raced to the cabin's front door and flung it open. Her face was swollen and bruised, and her lip was bleeding. She was halfway outside when she was jerked backward by an unshaven brute of a man with eyes inflamed by whiskey. He knocked Elizabeth onto the floor and kicked her hard in the side. As she struggled to crawl to a corner of the shabby, one-room shack, she struck a table filled with dishes, food, and a kerosene lamp, and everything crashed to the floor.

The enraged man pulled a Barlow-style knife out of a hunk of cooked deer meat and advanced toward Elizabeth. Her eyes were wide with terror. She screamed as he slashed the left side of her face with the knife. Blood gushed everywhere. He lunged again, and Elizabeth used all her strength to punch him in the throat. The crazed man dropped the knife and grabbed at his neck. His knees buckled and he gasped for air. Elizabeth quickly made her way to the stone fireplace and snatched a long iron rod, the end of which had been lying in the fire and was red hot. She held the piece of metal out in front of her, ready to strike the man should he get on his feet again and come after her.

Elizabeth was a fountain of blood as she ran again to the door. The injured man caught her leg before she could leave, and she hit him over the head with the iron rod. He let go and slowly sank to the floor. Elizabeth awaited his next attack, but he was motionless. She threw the iron rod down next to the table and the spilled kerosene. The hot poker ignited the liquid and set the table on fire. Panicked, Elizabeth bolted from the cabin.

Low-hanging branches tore at Elizabeth's arms and bleeding face as she fled through the forest. A flash of light and the sound of roaring flames startled her; she turned to see the cabin engulfed in fire. The man staggered out of the cabin, terribly burned. She watched in horror as he collapsed. He was dead.

Elizabeth "Betsey" Fail was born in Purgatory Swamp, Illinois, in the fall of 1807. She was the youngest of Abraham and Sarah Fail's seven children, and history records her life as difficult from the moment she entered the world. The Fails were poor farmers. The land near the Wabash River where they lived was stubborn and could be subdued only with vigorous cultivation. Crops were often washed away by floodwaters or overtaken by insects. Abraham struggled to keep his family clothed and fed. By the time Elizabeth turned eight, her parents decided that anyone in the home unable to work the fields would have to go. A peddler traveling through Lawrence County in 1815 offered to take Elizabeth. Sarah agreed but demanded a cast-iron skillet and five pounds of lard in exchange for her daughter. The green-eyed, auburn-haired girl scarcely understood what the peddler expected of her when she was traded again to another man at a makeshift camp near the Embarras River in southeastern Illinois. Elizabeth's new guardian was a gambler who mistreated her. After several years of being abused, she fought back. And now, smoldering next to the cabin, her abuser was dead.

After escaping the cabin, Elizabeth hid herself in the woods along the river. In time, the deep cuts on her face healed; a long scar that extended from her left cheekbone to the center of her chin bore witness to the struggles she had endured. She made her way back to civilization, finding employment at a boarding house in Logansport, Indiana, some 180 miles from the place where she was born. The establishment was a frequent stop for immigrants traveling up and down the Wabash and Eel Rivers that converged near town. Historians speculate this is where she met her first husband, John Stone. The couple were married for ten years. Stone held a series of odd jobs. Elizabeth educated herself in the practice of midwifery and learned how to cure a variety of ailments using herbs and other natural remedies. Quiet and aloof, she kept her pale and scarred face covered with a bonnet and handkerchief-style veil. Her conspicuous manner of dress and reserved demeanor made her a mysterious figure to those with whom she came in contact.

It is not known how old Elizabeth was when John left her, only that she returned to Lawrence County after he departed. She then met and married Leonard Reed, a native of Barren County, Kentucky, who owned a small farm south of Palestine, Illinois. Leonard was described as a "thin, frail man with salt-and-pepper hair, an oversized nose and a perpetual smile." Born in 1795, Leonard was twelve years older than Elizabeth. In addition to raising wheat and corn, he was also a trapper. The pair lived in a rustic cabin, and few people knew much about the Reeds' personal life, aside from sixteen-year-old Eveline Deal, described by various accounts as either a friendly neighbor or, more likely, Leonard's niece.

Most in the community found Elizabeth to be peculiar. Because she concocted medicinal treatments using tree bark, the internal organs of animals, and other nostrums—and because she kept her face mostly hidden—some believed she was a witch. Then in the summer of 1844, people wondered why they had not seen Leonard working his land or tending to his traps, and rumors flew that Elizabeth had put a hex on him to make him violently ill. Leonard was in fact sick, but Eveline told curious neighbors that dark magic was not to blame. However, she did suspect her aunt was responsible. Eveline claimed that Elizabeth and her uncle had quarreled and that Elizabeth had poisoned him.

After Leonard languished for three days, Dr. James Logan was called to the home to examine him. The doctor determined Leonard was close to death but could not find a reason for his declining health. He prescribed Leonard some medicine and asked his wife and niece to make sure he took it.

Dr. Logan promised to call on his patient again in a few days to monitor his condition. Eveline sat beside her uncle on the bed and dabbed beads of sweat off his tortured face with a damp cloth. Elizabeth prepared a pot of sassafras tea and helped her husband drink a cup of the brew. His situation did not improve. He died on August 19, 1844.

Leonard's funeral was reportedly well attended. Neighbors expressed their sympathy to his widow. Elizabeth nodded politely but said very little about her husband and his passing. After the ceremony she returned to the cabin alone. She barely had time to adjust to life without Leonard when Eveline publicly accused her aunt of poisoning her uncle, claiming she had witnessed the crime. The teen told law enforcement officials that Elizabeth slipped some white powder into Leonard's tea. Eveline suspected the powder to be arsenic, and she gave police a small piece of butcher paper she said had contained the deadly powder. When tested by authorities, the paper proved to have contained arsenic.

Elizabeth looked on in silence as Eveline guided the sheriff and his deputies into the cabin and explained what happened the fateful night her uncle died. She told the men that her aunt kept paper filled with arsenic in the cupboard. Eveline explained that after Elizabeth deposited the fatal dose into Leonard's tea, she tossed the paper out of the cabin. Her suspicions greatly aroused, Eveline says she snuck outside after dark and retrieved the paper. The authorities searched the crude home thoroughly and found additional pieces of paper similar to those that Eveline had discovered, each with a small amount of arsenic left inside.

According to court records, two county physicians exhumed and examined Leonard's body; they determined he had died as a result of chronic arsenic poisoning. For the physicians to establish that he had been poisoned, they had to convert body tissue and fluids into arsenic gas. They determined that Leonard was poisoned over the course of a week and died in great agony. The doctors' report combined with Eveline's statement was enough for authorities to arrest Elizabeth.

Further investigation led to the discovery of additional evidence. The druggist at a mercantile in Russellville, Illinois, came forward to say that he remembered selling Elizabeth the poison. He claimed she was in disguise when she came into the store, but authorities believe he mistook her natural state of dress, the low-hanging bonnet and kerchief-style veil over her face, as a disguise.

Court records show that all evidence compiled by authorities was presented to a grand jury, and they found that Elizabeth was responsible for Leonard's death. According to their report, "Elizabeth Reed, not having the fear of God before her eyes but being moved and seduced by the instigation of the Devil, had murdered her husband with a mixture of white arsenic and sassafras tea." The motivation for the crime was not clear, but Elizabeth did nothing to refute the case against her. She offered no defense and refused to speak to anyone who asked her questions. Public sentiment was not in her favor, either. Many of the people in the area saw her as cold-blooded and unfeeling. They didn't doubt she murdered Leonard.

Elizabeth was held at a jail in Palestine, Illinois. An angry crowd gathered outside the jail and demanded that the authorities release Elizabeth so they could lynch her. She watched the scene impassively from her cell window, never voicing an objection.

However, it soon became clear that she was desperate to escape the ordeal. The proof came when she attempted to break out of jail by setting fire to the building. The blaze was subdued before Elizabeth could get away. Deputies who had searched her before placing her in the cell were bewildered as to how she could have started the blaze. They said she had no access to anything that could set off even a spark. When news spread through Palestine that she apparently started a fire from nothing, residents were all the more convinced Elizabeth was a witch. Court records note residents believed Elizabeth was "practicing in the art of the occult and had summoned flames from the pit of hell."

People were afraid of Elizabeth; her attorneys, August French and Usher Linder, did not believe they could find any impartial individuals in Palestine to serve on a jury. They petitioned the court for a change of venue. While waiting for it to be granted, authorities kept Elizabeth chained to a bed in the sheriff's cabin. Since the jail had burned down there was no other place to keep prisoners. After a wait of more than nine months, Elizabeth was transferred to Lawrenceville. The prosecution and defense teams estimated the hearing would take three days to complete. Judge William Wilson oversaw the case, and the prosecuting attorney was Aaron Shaw. Wilson owned several farms near Carmi, Illinois, and was a well-respected chief justice of the Illinois Supreme Court, frequently presiding over cases featuring an up-and-coming young lawyer named Abraham Lincoln.

News of Elizabeth's trial spread throughout Illinois and even reached papers in New York. People followed the case closely as it progressed. According to the court records, witnesses testifying against Elizabeth were James Logan as the attending physician, Eveline Deal, and the two physicians who examined Leonard after his death. Logan was the first to take the stand when the trial started in late April 1845. He told the jury that Leonard died of "inflammation of the stomach, induced by some poisonous drug." He reported that when he examined Elizabeth's husband the day he passed away, his stomach was in a state of "incipient mortification." Although he had no personal knowledge that Elizabeth purchased arsenic from the store in Russellville, he felt certain she did acquire poison from the location.

Eveline Deal's statement about Elizabeth's actions leading up to her uncle's alleged murder proved to be most damning. "I saw Mrs. Reed take a small paper of white powder and she put it in a cup of sassafras tea and she gave it to Mr. L. Reed," she testified. "That seemed to make him very sick and caused him to vomit immediately . . . she emptied the powder from the paper. I believe she intended to throw it out of the door but it fell on the doorstep. I took up the paper and looked between two glass tea plates that sat in the cupboard and the same place that I saw her take the powder from and there I found another paper . . . the same kind of paper . . . along with pieces of an old book leaf that was considerably smoked. The first opportunity I gave them [the pieces of paper] to authorities."

Once Eveline left the stand, the two physicians who examined Leonard after his demise were called to tell what they knew. Both testified that Leonard's death was caused by the ingestion of arsenic. Court records do not show that anyone was called to defend Elizabeth. She was not allowed to take the stand because her lawyer felt she might incriminate herself. However, she vehemently declared her innocence from the defendant's table where she sat during the trial. She interrupted the prosecution several times when they accused her of killing Leonard Reed, insisting she had nothing to do with his death. Some courtroom spectators groaned disapprovingly.

No amount of protesting could sway the opinion of the judge and the all-male jury. On April 29, 1845, Elizabeth was found guilty of murder and sentenced to be hanged. Confined to the small jail cell until the date of her hanging on May 23, 1845, Elizabeth found the wait to be intolerable. In an effort to expedite her death, she began eating rocks and pieces of mortar from the cell walls, which only made her sick.

Just after daybreak on May 23, 1845, Elizabeth was led on a wagon to the gallows, located a mile from the courthouse where her trial had been held. According to eyewitnesses at the scene, Elizabeth wore a long, white robe given to her by the local minister and his wife. The garment was reported to have once belonged to one of the members of a religious sect known as the Millerites, who lived and worshipped in the Lawrenceville area. They believed the second coming of Christ was to occur in 1843 and made white robes for their journey to heaven. When the event failed to pass, the group disbanded. The minister who attended to Elizabeth's spiritual needs during her incarceration felt it was fitting she wear one of the robes when she died. It was his contention that Elizabeth had "confessed her crimes to him, sought and was granted forgiveness from the creator."

An astounding 20,000 people gathered from southern Illinois and neighboring Indiana to witness the execution. They watched Elizabeth arrive, seated on the very coffin in which she was to be buried. It was a bright and balmy morning, and Elizabeth was singing hymns of praise as she was led to the gallows.

John Seed, a well-known Methodist preacher, delivered a ninety-minute sermon to the crowd of onlookers about the need for their salvation. At the conclusion of the message, a noose was placed around Elizabeth's neck and a black hood was draped over her head. When the executioner pulled the lever and opened the trapdoor, the accused fell to her death. An eyewitness noted that she "revolved several times, but did not struggle much." Elizabeth Reed was the first and only woman executed by hanging in Illinois.

After Elizabeth's hanging, the community continued to speculate about Elizabeth's motive for poisoning her husband. Some insisted she was involved with another man and wanted Leonard out of the way so she could live a new life. Some speculated that Leonard found out Elizabeth was an outlaw who had murdered a man and burned his remains, and still others maintained it was Leonard who was involved with another, and Elizabeth had caught him in the act.

Elizabeth was buried next to her husband in a simply marked plot outside the Lawrenceville cemetery. ⇒

Elizabeth and Leonard Reed were buried together in a plot marked only by a simple stone. COURTESY OF ROGER CREED

A later tombstone describes the death of each of the Reeds. Elizabeth Reed became the first, and only, woman to be hanged in the state of Illinois. COURTESY OF ROGER CREED

CHAPTER THREE

KATE BENDER

A Woman Most Bloodthirsty

A fierce wind blasted alkali dust at Silas Toles, a farmer in Labette County, Kansas, as he made his way to his neighbor's seemingly vacant home. Three other farmers followed him tentatively. As they approached the weather-beaten building, they saw a hungry calf languishing in a nearby fenced enclosure, bawling piteously for something to eat. The calf had been bawling all day. Silas had heard the animal and called his neighbors together to go with him to find out what was wrong. In addition to the distressed and dehydrated calf, a handful of dead chickens lay scattered about the parched earth near the house.

The front door was ajar and creaked back and forth in the wind. Silas stood in the dirt entryway and glanced inside. Light from the late-afternoon sun filtered through partially drawn curtains onto the shabby furnishings in the center of the one-room home. The house was in complete disarray: clothing, books, paper, and dishes were on the floor; bugs covered bits of food on a broken table; chairs were overturned; and a pungent smell of death hung in the air.

The sound of fast-approaching horses distracted the quartet, and they watched as several riders raced to the spot and quickly dismounted.

Colonel A. M. York, a distinguished, bearded man dressed in the uniform of an Army officer, led a team of Civil War veterans and lawmen to the entrance of the home. They pushed past Silas and the others and boldly entered the house.

Colonel York surveyed the room, kicking away debris at his feet as he walked around. He wore a determined, yet forlorn expression. The group inspected the items carefully. They found a collection of pagan artifacts, including a pentagram and tarot cards, in the corner of the room. Some of the articles were covered with dried blood. Colonel York followed a trail of blood to a mound of fresh earth under a pile of soiled sheets. Kneeling down, he felt through the dirt until he uncovered a crude door. The men stared wide-eyed, waiting to see what the Colonel would do next. One of the lawmen stepped up and brushed the dirt away from a round handle attached to the door. Before giving it a pull, the man glanced over at the Colonel to see if he wanted to continue the search. The Colonel was quietly transfixed by the scene. The lawman interpreted his silence as an affirmative answer and quickly pulled the door open. The foul stench that wafted out of the dark hole hit the men like a punch in the face.

Colonel York stood and walked over to a trio of kerosene lamps sitting under a window. He lit them all and handed two to a nearby lawman, who handed one to another member of the group. Sweating profusely, the Colonel lowered himself into the hole.

The air reeked of death, and the men covered their noses and mouths with their kerchiefs. But for the sound of the men's careful footsteps, all was silent and still. Suddenly, Colonel York's foot caught on something; he froze. He held the lantern over the area where his boot made contact with the object and saw the torso of a man lying before him. The body was face down in a pool of dried blood.

"Is it your brother?" one of the men asked. Colonel York offered no response as he bent down next to the corpse. The back of the dead man's skull had been punctured and brain matter oozed from the wound. The Colonel rolled the body over. The deceased's eyes were open and his throat had been cut from ear to ear.

"Is it him?" The question was asked of Colonel York again.

"No," the Colonel finally responded. He stretched out his arm, lifting the lantern high and illuminating the far corner of the room. There were four more bodies. The Colonel instructed the members of his group who were waiting upstairs to remove the bodies, then paused to study the gory scene. Shock and horror registered on his face, and he was speechless.

It was April 1873 when Colonel York and his posse of volunteers searched the forsaken Kansas house. He had come searching for his brother, William H. York, a doctor who resided in Independence, Kansas. In March, the doctor had traveled to Fort Scott to visit the Colonel; on his way home to his wife and practice he went missing. According to the Colonel, his brother was dressed in a fine suit, carried a gold pocket watch, and had a large sum of money with him when he left for home. His horse and saddle were of the finest quality. When last seen, Dr. York was riding toward a stage stop known as the Bender House. Acquaintances who saw the doctor on the road told Colonel York his brother had planned to have dinner at the Bender House and continue on. That was the last anyone saw of him.

The Bender House stage stop, located seven miles northeast of Cherryvale, one hundred yards from the main road, opened to the public in 1871. It was owned and operated by a German family from Pennsylvania, sixty-one-year-old John Bender, his wife Katherine, their twenty-year-old daughter Kate, and son John Jr., twenty-seven years old. Kate was a statuesque figure with dark hair and coal-black eyes. Of the four, she was the most social. She readily engaged with neighbors and passersby and had a pleasing sense of humor. Kate and her mother dabbled in the occult. They made regular visits to the sick in the county and claimed to be able to cure their infirmities by reciting incantations. Kate's venture into such spiritualism was the subject of a stage act she performed in various Kansas towns. Billed as "Professor Miss Katie Bender," she performed séances and convinced audiences to pay her large sums to deliver messages to their loved ones who had passed on.

Kate and her mother managed to make superstitious Labette County residents believe they possessed the power to locate lost objects. For a five dollar consulting fee, the Bender women would listen to the particulars of the misplaced item, pretend to contact the mischievous spirit that took the item, and reveal where it was hidden. Desperate to find missing loved ones, friends and family called upon Kate to advise authorities where to look for those who had disappeared. Kate often told poor souls who sought her

Kate Bender and her family ran a stage stop in Kansas. She was a dark-haired, social beauty with a thirst for blood.

professional expertise that the missing people were alive and well and on their way to the Indian Territory, Texas, or some other not-too-distant region. She was able to convey the misleading information with emotion and conviction worthy of a theatrical starlet.

The Bender House, where the sinister family lived, offered food and lodging to weary travelers making their way across the prairie to homesteads west of the Mississippi. Horses and wagons were placed in a barn not far from the crude house. John and his son cared for the animals. Kate and her mother made the meals and prepared a place for guests to sleep. Before retiring for the evening, Kate would regale patrons with fortune-telling or palm-reading. Somewhere in the middle of the act, her brother or father would give her a signal that indicated they believed customers had money.

Kate Bender took the name Professor Miss Katie Bender and advertised her so-called healing powers to con money from her customers. The knife in this photo was found in the Bender house. The Bender men would bludgeon their victims, and once they were unconscious, Kate would slit their throats. KANSAS STATE HISTORICAL SOCIETY

A secretive but thorough inspection of the travelers' personal belongings enabled the family patriarch and his son to determine how much the guests had on them. The value of the horses they rode and quality of the wagons they brought with them was also taken into consideration. The plan was to keep the overnight visitors distracted long enough for one of the men to get behind them and hit them in the head. Once they were unconscious, Kate would cut their throats and take their money and personal belongings. The victims were then deposited in a pit under the house and later buried.

During Colonel York's first sweep through the region in search of his brother, he enlisted the help of Kate's brother and father. John Bender told the Colonel and his party that he believed the doctor might have been attacked by a group of wild bandits that had been terrorizing the region. Kate agreed with her father and told the Colonel that Doctor York had been a guest at their business. She added that he had ridden out the following morning in the direction of a spot known as Drum Creek.

Having no reason to doubt the young woman, Colonel York led the searchers to the area described. John Bender and his son rode along with the group and, once they arrived at the spot to be searched, helped comb the shallow waterbed for a body. The collection of men aiding Colonel York in his efforts to find his brother disbanded after only the remains of a hog were uncovered. The Benders returned to their home, and the Colonel rode on to a nearby town to continue the search. In reviewing the difficult country he had traveled and the people he had met along the way, his thoughts settled on Kate and her family. There were many similarities in the way father and daughter told the story of the thieving bandits, as if it were rehearsed. The Colonel was suspicious and decided to question the family again. Eleven days after he first visited the stage stop, Colonel York returned with a larger group of men to help him find out what happened to his brother. And it was on that day in April that he made the gruesome discovery beneath the abandoned Bender House.

Now shaken, but determined, Colonel York scanned the ground around the Bender House. Beyond the barn he noticed a garden and an orchard, neither of which were very well maintained. Weeds grew between several rows of corn; rotten tomatoes littered the ground beneath dying plants. Dirt was heaped in narrow mounds in front of a stand of neglected apple trees. Colonel

York's face grew pale as he realized what the heaped dirt represented. "Boys," he said to the men with him, "I see graves yonder in the orchard."

Colonel York removed the ramrod from his military rifle and plunged it into the first mound he came to. He struck something. The colonel slowly raised the ramrod to the surface and inspected it. Human hair was on the end of the tool. He repeated the process at the next grave and drew out a piece of clothing. Colonel York tossed the ramrod aside, dropped to his knees, and quickly began to paw at the dirt. He ordered the stunned men with him to find shovels and spades and start digging; they quickly obeyed.

The first body they uncovered was a man. Like the one in the basement of the house, this one, too, had a deep gash in the back of the skull and a slashed throat. When they were done, the men had uncovered nine bodies from the garden and orchard. Not a word was exchanged as the group performed the gruesome task of removing the bodies from their shallow graves and placing them side by side. A few wept when the corpse of a little girl was discovered among the dead. Colonel York was moved to tears when he identified his brother among the murder victims. Doctor York's skull had been crushed on the right side. He'd been stripped of his fine clothing, and his pocket watch was gone.

Colonel York and the lawmen at the scene determined that Kate Bender and her family must have preyed on vulnerable solitary riders. The unsuspecting Bender House customers were ushered into the establishment and seated at a table next to a curtain that divided the spacious room in half. They were served a meal, and, while they ate, John Jr. tended to their horses and rifled through their possessions in their saddlebags. At some point in the evening, one of the Bender men would position himself behind the curtain and strike the guests on the head with a hammer. Kate then descended upon them and sliced their throats open from ear to ear with a razor-edged knife. The deceased were tossed into a pit under the home and left there until the Bender men could bury them in the orchard. The wagons, horses, harnesses, and saddles that belonged to the murder victims were sold to Native Americans in the area, who resold the items at trading posts in the West. A confession later made by Katherine Bender to U.S. Marshals and published by the *Chicago Evening Journal* on July 30, 1880, confirmed York's and the lawmen's scenario of the crimes.

An excavated grave of a victim of Kate Bender. The grave was found under a trapdoor at the Bender House. Bodies of the Bender victims were stored under the house until the Bender men could bury them in the orchard. KANSAS STATE HISTORICAL SOCIETY

The disappearance of wayward travelers had not gone unnoticed. Occasionally a friend or family member passed through the area, searching for the missing. But it wasn't until Colonel York and his men came through that residents in southeast Kansas began to realize that something horrific had been taking place in their midst. Ten out of the fourteen bodies were eventually identified. A grave filled with dismembered body parts was also discovered, but the charred remains were identifiable only as human.

Among those who were acquainted with the Benders, either because they were neighbors or had sold them goods at the store in Cherryvale, the consensus was that the Benders fled the area under cover of darkness. The theory was echoed by Rudolph Brockman, a neighbor who had courted Kate for a short time. Brockman admitted to proposing marriage to Kate, but they could not agree on a date to tie the knot. "She showed me a number of complicated astrological charts to support the day we should be wed but the proper nuptial conjunction never fell into place," Brockman confessed to authorities.

Brockman did not know Kate and her family had fled the area until searchers besieged him with questions about his relationship with the family. The posse that helped question Brockman was not entirely pleased with his answers. They did not believe he was unaware of the Benders' murderous actions or that he didn't know their whereabouts. The angry mob fashioned a noose around a tree and hanged Brockman by the neck. Before he expired, friends cut him down and revived him.

Kansas Governor Thomas Osborn took immediate action when he learned of the grisly murders. A 2,000 dollar reward was posted for each member of the Bender family—dead or alive.

Colonel York was heartbroken over the brutal killing of his brother. He wanted to see the Benders dead. Every gypsy family or small band of prospectors or trappers making their way through the area of Cherryvale was cornered and questioned by York and his lawmen about whether they'd seen anyone matching the Benders' description. No one had come in contact with the family.

Colonel York estimated that Kate, her brother, and her parents had left the area on April 29, 1873, heading north. He concluded that the country in that direction would be most ideal for them because it was sparsely settled and the roads were less traveled. The Benders would be better able to make their way around without being detected.

Colonel York and the posse followed a lead on the family that took them into the Indian Territory in what is now Oklahoma. They pursued rumors of sightings of the Benders from one end of the territory to the other. By the fall of 1873, posse members believed Kate Bender and her family had escaped to Dennison, Texas, and that they were working with a railroad construction gang. But the posse was weary, and the long search effort was losing steam. Colonel York could not convince the majority of the posse to venture on with him. They were tired and disillusioned and decided to return to their homes. Colonel York was left with a handful of men to see the search through to

GOVERNOR'S PROCLAMATION.

$2,000 REWARD

State of Kansas, Executive Department.

WHEREAS, several atrocious murders have been recently committed in Labette County, Kansas, under circumstances which fasten, beyond doubt, the commissions of these crimes upon a family known as the "Bender family," consisting of

JOHN BENDER, about 60 years of age, five feet eight or nine inches in height, German, speaks but little English, dark complexion, no whiskers, and sparely built;

MRS. BENDER, about 50 years of age, rather heavy set, blue eyes, brown hair, German, speaks broken English;

JOHN BENDER, Jr., alias John Gebardt, five feet eight or nine inches in height, slightly built, gray eyes with brownish tint, brown hair, light moustache, no whiskers, about 27 years of age, speaks English with German accent;

KATE BENDER, about 24 years of age, dark hair and eyes, good looking, well formed, rather bold in appearance, fluent talker, speaks good English with very little German accent:

AND WHEREAS, said persons are at large and fugitives from justice, now therefore, I, Thomas A. Osborn, Governor of the State of Kansas, in pursuance of law, do hereby offer a REWARD OF FIVE HUNDRED DOLLARS for the apprehension and delivery to the Sheriff of Labette County, Kansas, of each of the persons above named.

In Testimony Whereof, I have hereunto subscribed my name, and caused the Great Seal of the State to be affixed.

[L. S.]   Done at Topeka, this 17th day of May, 1873.

THOMAS A. OSBORN,
Governor.

By the Governor:

W. H. SMALLWOOD,
Secretary of State.

A reward poster for Kate Bender and other members of her family—wanted dead or alive—issued in 1873 by Kansas Governor Thomas Osborn. KANSAS STATE HISTORICAL SOCIETY

the end. He needed to report back to Fort Scott before he continued on but didn't want the trail to grow cold. He hired three professional trackers to race ahead to Texas. The men were given 1,000 dollars for their efforts, and all their expenses were taken care of as well. Although the trackers were exceptional at their jobs, Texas authorities were less than helpful. They refused to let the men search the territory for individuals, who, as far as they knew, had committed no crimes in Texas. The trackers returned to Kansas empty-handed.

Leroy F. Dick, an associate of the Benders, claimed in his memoir that John Sr. and his wife fled to Michigan. Kate and her brother John Jr. disappeared somewhere into the Southwest. Leroy F. Dick maintains that John Jr. eventually killed himself when he realized there was no escaping public scrutiny. Articles in the *Chicago Evening Journal*, and on August 13, 1880, in the *Warren* [Pennsylvania] *Ledger* substantiated some of the information about the Benders contained in Dick's journal. According to the newspaper accounts, patriarch John Bender was arrested near Fremont, Nebraska, on July 30, 1880. He and his wife Katherine, who had been traveling together on foot, had stopped at a road house for supplies and while they were there asked if anyone knew about the Bender family and if they had ever been caught. The odd question and John's behavior aroused suspicion, and the sheriff was notified. The couple was arrested and placed in jail until the law could make sense of their peculiar query.

John and his wife were locked in a cell together, and one of the jailers overheard a conversation between the two involving the desire to lay hands on a sharp object in order to commit suicide. "I know if they send us back to Kansas they'll hang us before we're there two hours," they overheard John saying. "We would not stand a ghost of a show. If I have to die I want to die with you and be buried with you," he told his wife. The two discussed how they would kill themselves if they were able to acquire a razor. John theorized that the guards would never let them have such an item. "They are afraid of losing their reward," he told his despondent spouse. Fearing the pair would contrive a method to do away with themselves, the police separated them. When John asked authorities where they were taking his wife, they told him they were taking her to Kansas. In truth she was being held at another location well away from her husband and questioned thoroughly about the murders that took place in the Bender home.

According to the *Warren Ledger* and the *Chicago Evening Journal*, Katherine Bender finally told her side of the gruesome events after several hours of interrogation. "I was with the old man [my husband] all the time," she told the lawmen. "The money taken from persons murdered was always divided. The garden was full of graves and the cellar full of bodies. Colonel York's brother was murdered while I was there. He was a single man, I think, about thirty-five years old. He was such a pleasant man, with side whiskers and a moustache. It was a rainy day when he came and they got a good deal of money when they killed him. He fought hard, too, but Kate killed him with a hatchet. I think there were more than ten people killed while I was there."

The *Warren Ledger* article also noted that when the authorities told John what his wife revealed he decided to confess, too. "Individuals would stop by the house to get something to eat," he explained to the authorities. "A young man from California that came by wanted to know why the house smelled so. Kate told him it was nothing. I don't think the man believed her. He told her he wasn't going to stay the night. Kate and John Junior had put two children in the hole earlier that day and covered them with dirt. The man from California was the man that saw the children when they were alive. When Kate and John Junior saw they'd been found out they left right then. I went to Jacksonville, Illinois, by foot, called myself McGregor. Don't know where the others went. About four weeks after we left the house I saw Kate between Springfield, Illinois, and Jacksonville. She had men's clothes on. She had her hair cut short."

After several hours of being questioned, John grew quiet and sullen. "I don't care what they do to me," he concluded.

Leroy Dick insists in his published recollections that John Bender finally did manage to get hold of a sharp object and cut his own throat. Some historians have reported that the authorities allowed an angry mob entry into the jail and that John and his wife Katherine were taken and killed and their bodies secretly disposed of. Most historians believe the pair broke out of jail and escaped justice.

Two women believed to be Kate Bender and her mother Katherine were arrested at a small town in southern Kansas in 1888. Mrs. Frances McPherson and Sara Eliza Davis were charged with the murder of Dr. York and held over for trial. They were acquitted after key witnesses failed to positively identify the pair as the Benders.

On March 12, 1890, Frank Ayers, a cattle rancher from Colorado, traveled to Labette County, Kansas, with news that he had located Kate and John Jr. Not only did he claim the pair was living in Longmont, Colorado, and had changed their names to Baker, but also that Kate Bender was once his wife. Ayers told police he was Kate's third husband. The first had deserted her and the second had died in prison.

According to the *Milford Mail*, a newspaper in Milford, Iowa, in an article on June 18, 1901, Ayers and Kate moved to Fort Collins shortly after they were married. John Jr. decided to remain in Longmont, where he owned a string of racehorses and worked at a livery stable. "Our troubles began once I moved her into the house I had built for her," Ayers told authorities. "One night my coffee was drugged and I knew nothing more for fourteen days. When I recovered I was in the Baker home [a boardinghouse in Manhattan, Colorado, where the couple lived when they first met] and informed that a friend had found me on the railroad tracks. I had been hit in the back of the head." The friend that had found Ayers took him to the Baker house where he was nursed back to health by his wife, the alleged Kate Bender.

Ayers told the police he was placed on the railroad tracks with the "expectation that a train would finish him, but the timely aid of an old friend saved him." He believed his wife nursed him back to health to avoid suspicion. He noted that even after his friend rescued him, some of his medicines were poisoned, and his friend threw them away. Ayers claimed that after his recovery he made inquiries and was convinced that he had been foully dealt with by his wife, and so he deserted her.

Ayers soon had further confirmation of his suspicions. He had long believed that the ranch he owned in Colorado had oil beneath it, and he sent a man out to look at it. This man had lived in Labette County, Kansas, when the Bender murders were committed, and knew the Benders. Upon the man's return he told Ayers that he had seen Kate Bender. He said Kate Ayers and Kate Bender were one and the same; another man who was sent to Colorado on a separate matter returned with the same story. Despite the fact that seven witnesses verified Ayers' wife as Kate Bender, Labette County authorities refused to act on the matter.

More than seventeen years passed from the time the bodies of the four-teen murder victims were found at the Bender home until the time the police discussed reexamining the case. The crime was so gruesome, however, that investigators decided not to revisit the incident.

From 1890 to 1909, rumors of the Benders' whereabouts circulated from one small Midwestern town to another. Some believed Colonel York eventu-ally tracked down Kate and John Jr. and shot them dead. Others thought the family fled to Mexico never to be seen or heard from again. On May 6, 1910, the *New York Times* reported that Kate Bender died at the inn she ran in Rio Vista, California. Area resident John Collins notified the press of the notori-ous woman's demise. "The woman, who was known as Mrs. Gavin, and later as Mrs. Peters, was found dead in a resort she conducted," the article read. "Collins, who was her friend, said she revealed her identity to him several years ago, exacting a promise that he should not tell anybody until after her death. The woman apparently died from natural causes, and had been dead several days when her body was found. Collins declared that she gave him a detailed account of many murders which she and her brother committed in the Bender home at Cherryvale, Kansas, in the seventies." As there was no one to identify the deceased as truly being Kate Bender, Collins' claim was largely ignored.

What really became of Kate Bender, her parents, and her brother remains a mystery. Criminologists investigating the case in 1911 told the *Washington Post* that Kate Bender was "one of the most fiendish female murderers in his-tory." They speculated that her end probably came at the hand of a victim who successfully fought back. ⊷

CHAPTER FOUR

FANNIE & JENNIE FREEMAN

The Railroad Fakirs

Nineteen-year-old Jennie Freeman* stared pensively out the partially opened window of the tenement building where she lived in Chicago, Illinois. A cold, gentle breeze blew across the bed where she sat, and she pulled at the dingy blankets draped across her legs. Jennie was a petite, spectacled girl with mousey-brown hair and green eyes. She was an avid reader, proven by the many books stacked around the bed. A stern-faced doctor stood over her, fiddling with a stethoscope. When he finally placed one end of the stethoscope on Jennie's chest, she turned her attention from the street scene to him. The doctor listened to his patient's heartbeat, then scratched his head, perplexed. He eyed the wheelchair next to the bed and let out a heavy sigh. Jennie's mother, Fannie, entered the room from the kitchen, carrying a tray of food. She was a large woman of dark complexion who wore diamond eardrops and a large marquise ring. She looked worried and carefully studied the doctor's face, waiting for him to speak.

The doctor lifted the covers off Jennie's legs and examined her feet. He removed a straight pin from his medical bag and touched it to Jennie's foot and calves. No matter what he did, he could not get her limbs to even twitch. After a few quiet moments, he pulled the blanket back over Jennie's legs and began packing up his medical instruments. Fannie grasped her daughter's hand. The doctor confirmed what the troubled mother had suspected—Jennie was paralyzed. As the doctor put on his coat and exited the cramped, poorly lit home, Fannie held Jennie as the girl sobbed.

Jennie suffered her injury when she got caught between two cable cars. The intricate system of street railways in downtown Chicago had malfunctioned on January 9, 1893, and the cars collided. Jennie was found on the ground writhing in pain. After a short stay in the hospital to treat her cracked ribs, bruises, and cuts, she was released into the care of her mother. Two days later she was unable to move her legs from the thighs down. A railway company physician verified the report. Believing it would be cheaper to settle than it would be to go to court, the company paid Jennie 500 dollars. By October 5, 1893, Jennie Freeman began to recover, regaining use of her legs.

The following spring, Jennie Freeman was injured after riding the Manhattan Elevated Railroad in New York to her first stop. The woman told authorities she was an actress on her way to an audition when she fell against the door of a Second Avenue train while waiting to board the vehicle to her second stop. She told them the car swung too close to the corner she was standing on at Twenty-third Street. "I lost my balance and hit it hard," she reported. "The car was going too fast, too," she added. Her mother was on hand to back up the story. Jennie was awarded 100 dollars from the rail line for the injuries she claimed to have sustained, and Fannie was given 50 dollars for suffering. "Seeing my daughter go through that was horrible," she told the police at the scene of the accident.

On April 20, 1894, the Freemans were in Boston, Massachusetts, traveling aboard the West End Street Railway Company car. Jennie claimed to have slipped on a banana peel lying in the aisle of the car. She told law enforcement officials who responded to her emergency call that she couldn't move from the waist down. A doctor for the railway examined her and found her in a condition of apparent paralysis. As a result of the doctor's report, the West End Street Railway Company paid her 325 dollars.

On May 16, 1894, Jennie Freeman made a claim against the Cincinnati, Ohio, Railroad Company for alleged injuries received while getting off a company car. She again said she had stepped on a banana peel, which she produced in evidence. She accepted 125 dollars in settlement of the case.

On June 28, 1894, Jennie claimed to have been injured while boarding a train of the Illinois Central Railroad Company by, again, stepping on a banana peel, which threw her backwards against a seat. She alleged total insensibility of the lower part of her body, practically amounting to paralysis. A physician for the company did every possible test, even sticking pins into her legs, but she appeared totally insensitive to the pain. The company settled with her for 200 dollars.

Jennie and Fannie Freeman, the "Railroad Fakirs," as the newspapers referred to them, were two of the most accomplished and wanted women in the "false claims" business. The two were skilled at the art of staging "whiplash or other soft tissue injuries" that were hard to dispute later. Railway companies in the Midwest and on the East Coast, as well as cable car companies on the West Coast, believed the pair made more than 150,000 dollars from 1891 to 1894 by faking injuries.

In early July 1894, however, an unlucky coincidence nearly led to the duo's downfall. According to a later newspaper account, on July 6, 1894, one Elsie Deldon claimed her daughter had been injured on the New York, New Haven & Hartford Railroad by stepping on a banana peel just after the train arrived in Boston. "Now it just happened that Dr. R. P. Hubbard, who had called upon Jennie and Fannie Freeman for the West End Street Railway Company, was also the examining physician for the New York, New Haven & Hartford Railroad," the newspaper report read. When Dr. Hubbard came to examine Elsie Deldon's daughter, she was lying in bed, weeping. He immediately recognized the injured woman as Jennie Freeman. And she claimed to be suffering with the same symptoms as when he evaluated her the year before.

"The woman who let me into the house had been introduced to me in the past as Fannie," he later recalled for the paper. "But this time she said her name was Elsie. They both appeared not to recognize me and I played the same game with them. Jennie, or, as Elsie referred to her, Bella, complained she was paralyzed; she claimed to have never had any previous accidents, had never been confined to her bed since childhood; had never had a doctor call on her in her life; and her mother corroborated her statement. The mother pulled me aside and pleaded with me to heal her daughter. I told her

I didn't think Bella was seriously injured but that they needed to go to the Providence depot the following day to settle things up."

Dr. Hubbard was waiting for Fannie when she arrived at the depot the next morning. He told her that he knew who she was and offered her a piece of advice. He suggested that she and her daughter not steal from the rail lines in the Boston area again. The doctor told her he had notified every large corporation in the city about their actions and promised he would have them arrested if they came back.

Evidently the Freemans took the hint because they were back in Chicago that September—where Jennie attempted, without success, to make the West Chicago Street Railway pay for another faked paralysis episode. The very next day her mother claimed to have had her arm wrenched by a Chicago City Railway car and received 100 dollars for it.

The claim agent of the Cincinnati Railway was sitting in his office on December 24, 1894, when Fannie entered and informed him that her daughter had been injured while riding on one of the trains. She said it had left the station at 4:50 P.M. on December 10 and that a sudden start of the train had caused Jennie to fall, striking her back against a seat. As a result she had become paralyzed and ruined for life.

The claim agent told a news reporter that he had never heard of the Freemans, but in the course of the investigation he found several incongruities in the mother's statement that made him suspicious. For instance, no single-trip tickets had been punched by the conductor on duty, and the crew was positive that no sudden start had been made or was possible at the scene of the accident. Fannie insisted the accident did happen and that she and her daughter had saved themselves from falling by catching hold of the straps hanging in the cars. Fannie told the claim agent that her daughter's future invalidism was worth 2,000 dollars.

The Cincinnati Railway hired a private detective to look into the Freemans' claims. Detective Eugene Lawson, from Cleveland, took the case. He lost no time ingratiating himself with the Freeman ladies. Using the name "Mr. Seymour," he began to visit the Freemans often and became friends with Jennie. She was confined to her bed and claiming to be paralyzed. Lawson found that the family consisted of the mother, Jennie, five children under the age of ten, a father in Boston, and a son in New York. As friendly as he was with Jennie, Lawson could not find a chink in her masquerade of paralysis. Undeterred, he tried a more devious approach.

Lawson rented the apartment directly above the Freemans and moved in an employee of the rail line and his wife. Soon after their arrival, under the pretense that a rat had died in the flooring, a hole was cut in the back parlor directly above the spot where Jennie's bed was located. The dead rat "fell" into the room below, and the rail line employee ran down, apologizing for the mishap. He promised to have the hole repaired immediately; it was patched up, but an inconspicuous opening was left so that a person upstairs could peer through the hole while lying on the floor. So there might be no possibility of error, many people associated with the case were allowed to spy through the hole in the floor.

One Sunday in mid-January 1895, Detective Lawson and another employee with the rail company witnessed something critical to the case. According to a later account in the *San Antonio* [Texas] *Daily Light:*

> Fannie Freeman was sitting in a high-back dining chair at the foot of the bed. One of her daughters was sitting in a chair directly in front of a stove, and the other children were playing on the floor. Fannie, addressing Jennie lying in the bed, asked her what she had done with the shoes belonging to one of the children. Jennie told her that she had put them in the other room. She then asked Fannie to hand her the paper that was lying on the back of the bed. Fannie picked up the paper and handed it to her. Jennie then placed both her feet on the headboard of the bed and began reading the paper.
>
> At one o'clock in the afternoon, forty-five minutes before the doctor for the rail line was to arrive and examine Jennie, Fannie sat down at a piano and started to play a tune. Jennie got up and danced with her siblings. After five or ten minutes, Fannie left the room and reappeared carrying a large basin of ice water, into which she plunged Jennie's feet. Jennie kept her feet there almost until the very moment the physician arrived. She occasionally swore at the extreme coldness of the water, but her mother cheered her on and helped her to dry her feet quickly so she could become properly

rigid for the doctor's inspection. When the doctor arrived he was escorted into the home and he went about examining Jennie's feet and calves. No amount of prodding could make her limbs move.

Several hours after Lawson secretly witnessed the events at the Freemans' home, the police arrested the conspirators. Jennie and Fannie were tried, found guilty, and each sentenced to a year in prison. Upon their release from the Queens County Jail in New York in 1896, the pair relocated to Fort Worth, Texas, where the trail of the "fakirs" runs cold. ⊷

Although their names were spelled the same and their criminal actions took place around the same time, grifter Jennie Freeman and Jennie Freeman, the outlaw who ran with Zip Wyatt's gang (see Chapter 7), are two different, unrelated people.

"Railroad Fakirs" Jennie and Fannie Freeman are believed to have made more than $150,000 off railroad companies by faking injuries on cable cars similar to this one until their arrest in January 1895. PHOTOGRAPHER UNKNOWN

CHAPTER FIVE

SARAH QUANTRILL

Outlaw Bride

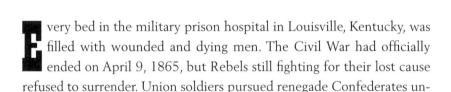

E very bed in the military prison hospital in Louisville, Kentucky, was filled with wounded and dying men. The Civil War had officially ended on April 9, 1865, but Rebels still fighting for their lost cause refused to surrender. Union soldiers pursued renegade Confederates until they were captured or shot.

Guerrilla leader William Quantrill and his followers were holed up in a barn on James H. Wakefield's farm in Spencer County, Kentucky. A Union ranger party tracked Quantrill down on May 10, 1865. A firefight broke out, and William was shot in the back while trying to flee the scene. The bullet struck the left side of his body near his shoulder blade and careened downward into his spine. The impact of the bullet knocked him off his horse, face down into the mud. William struggled to get to his feet but found he was completely paralyzed from the chest down.

The next thing the Confederate soldier knew he was lying in a crude, narrow bed. He winced in pain and attempted to reposition himself. The thin bandage placed over his wound did not stop the blood soaking through the top cover of dirty sheets. Seventeen-year-old Sarah Catherine King was seated next to him on the bed, trying to keep him still. She was a sturdy, buxom girl with striking features and raven-colored hair. She flashed a smile at the dying man, reached out, and gently took his hand in hers. The twenty-seven-year-old patient was pale, but his features were still sharp and handsome. With great effort he lifted his head to search the room for members of his loyal band of followers. A few kerosene lamps offered the only light in the room, and the place was swarming with flies. William's eyes came to rest on the form of a man lying in a blood-soaked bed next to him. The soon-to-be-dead man was crying like a child. William didn't know who he was. William did recognize Sarah, however. She was his wife.

When William looked at Sarah, tears of pain rolled down his face and sweat broke out on his forehead. She kissed his cheek. He was comforted by his wife's presence. Sarah explained to him that a priest had stopped by the boardinghouse she operated in St. Louis and let her know that "he had been wounded in a scuffle on a farm and was not expected to live."

Tears welled up in Sarah's eyes and spilled onto William's hand. With as much strength as he could manage he brushed the tears from her cheek. Stretcher carriers came and transported the dead man lying next to the couple away. The appalling conditions at the hospital as well as the sounds of the wounded swept over Sarah, and for a moment she sat frozen with the horror of the picture.

A priest approached the couple and in a low voice instructed Sarah to let him have some time with her husband. The clergyman wanted to pray with William and encourage him to get his heart right with his Maker. Sarah overheard a little of William's confession and watched him be baptized into the Catholic faith. William's child bride had been watching him languish in terrible pain for more than two days, but he suffered from his wounds for nearly a month. The Confederate soldier referred to as "the bloodiest man in the annals of America" breathed his last breath on June 6, 1865.

Sarah left town before her spouse of two-and-a-half years was dead and buried in the Portland Catholic Cemetery in Louisville. She suspected there would come a time when Union officers would look beyond her grieving and want to question her about what she knew of the property, jewelry, and cash her husband had taken from Lawrence, Kansas. Captain William Quantrill and his men had attacked the town in August 1863, killing hundreds and looting the businesses, banks, and homes before burning the town to the

Sarah King, later Kate Clarke, accompanied her husband, William Quantrill, and his guerrillas on raids against Union towns. JACKSON COUNTY (MO.) HISTORICAL SOCIETY ARCHIVES

ground. William had shared his spoils of war with his wife but told her to deny having any of the loot if she was ever asked. By the time authorities were ready to speak with Sarah about William's raids on Kansas, she was long gone. Law enforcement officials would seek her out in much the same way they did her outlaw husband.

Sarah Catherine King met William Clarke Quantrill at her parents' farm near Blue Springs, Missouri, in the winter of 1861. She was thirteen years old and William was twenty-three. More than a hundred of William's men had set up camp around Robert and Malinda King's homestead. While Robert and William were standing on the farmer's porch discussing the progress of the Civil War, Sarah arrived home from school and hurried to her father's side. As told by the *Fort Wayne Weekly Gazette* on August 31, 1888, Sarah was instantly smitten by the charming Confederate officer. He was handsome, had blue eyes, and carried himself with sincere self-assuredness. William admired Sarah as well. In a later *Kansas City Star* interview that ran on May 23, 1926, then eighty-one-year-old Sarah was described as "lively and jolly; a disposition which years of turmoil and suffering since had not changed. Old-timers who knew her remembered that she was pretty beyond question. She was raised on a farm. Her time spent mostly outdoors, and a great deal of that time spent horseback riding, had given her health and vigor and rosy cheeks. She could ride a horse like one born to the saddle. Ever since she was old enough to hold a rein her father had provided her with a mount, one that she could call her own."

William made frequent visits to the King homestead after his introduction to Sarah. He dined with her and her family, and they took long horseback rides together. Sarah's mother and father were concerned about the age difference between the two; just as the friendship was evolving into something more, Robert and Malinda King forbade Sarah from seeing William any longer. The strong-willed teenager and the insubordinate militia leader refused to obey. Their relationship continued in secret. Sarah snuck out of the house to meet William, and the pair enjoyed spending time talking about their lives and possibilities for the future.

Decades after William's death, Sarah told reporters at the *Kansas City Star* that he had been candid with her about his difficult upbringing and trouble with authority. William's family came from Hagerstown, Maryland. He was born at

Canal Dover, Ohio, on July 31, 1837. "I was a quiet, reserved boy," he told Sarah, who later shared details about him with the *Kansas City Star*. He had said, "I would fight if drawn into a brawl and felt I was obliged to defend myself, but it was not my choice to start trouble," the paper quoted her as saying.

William told Sarah that he was an exceptional marksman. "'Watch me make a pig squeal,' I would tell our neighbor Mr. Scott. Then I'd draw my gun and put a clean round hole through the ear of the pig twenty yards away." Tales of his childhood antics gave way to stories of becoming a teacher and potential landowner. "I was too young to enter an agreement with a bank to purchase property so neighbors did purchase the property on my behalf," he explained to Sarah. "After all the hard work I put in on the homestead the neighbors refused to turn the deed over to me. I was infuriated over the matter." William sought his revenge against the people who ultimately "took the land meant for him by stealing some of their livestock." He confessed to Sarah that he was arrested for the theft.

Shortly after his legal troubles ended, William moved to Kansas and taught school. He was content to continue teaching until he met abolitionist John Brown. William told Sarah that before the Civil War broke out and before he joined the Confederacy, he and friend John Brown made midnight raids across the border into Missouri to steal slaves from their owners and set them free. Sarah pressed to find out why he decided to fight for the South if he was against slavery. "An act of treachery" [changed his position], he replied. Shortly after the Civil War began, William and three fellow Union soldiers had planned to make a midnight raid on Morgan L. Walker, a rich farmer in Jackson County, Missouri, not far from Sarah's family's homestead. William rode ahead of the others to make sure the way was clear. When he entered Walker's house, the family kindly welcomed him and gave him dinner. The Walkers' hospitality caused him to reconsider his actions. Instead of returning to his comrades and carrying out the raid, William revealed the whole plot to Walker and his sons, even telling them where the men were hiding out. Heavily armed, Walker and one of his sons crept up on the raiders. The Walkers opened fire, and one of the raiders was killed. The other two temporarily escaped. They were eventually found and murdered.

William Quantrill, Morgan Walker, and his sons later joined forces. By December 1860, William was at the head of a powerful guerrilla band on the

Kate's husband, William Quantrill, led his group of 450 outlaw guerrilla warriors on a vicious massacre at the pro-Union town of Lawrence, Kansas, on August 21, 1863. The raid would leave 183 Lawrence residents dead and much of the city burned to the ground. JACKSON COUNTY (MO.) HISTORICAL SOCIETY ARCHIVES

side of the South. "When the war broke out my name was already a terror to free state Kansas," he told Sarah.

The very young and very naïve Sarah found William's candor refreshing. She spent every moment away from him devising ways to leave her family and make her life with the renegade. On one occasion a neighbor saw William and Sarah riding together near a creek. When her father learned that Sarah had disobeyed, he took her horse away from her. But not even that could stop her from seeing William. At the first opportunity she walked to his camp and explained what had occurred. Sarah told the *Kansas City Star* in 1926 that she and William decided then to marry. In the spring of 1861, William escorted her to the home of a country preacher six miles away and the pair exchanged vows. Their wedding night was spent in an abandoned cabin. William insisted she change her name to Kate Clarke (taking William's middle name as her last) in order to keep their relationship a secret from his enemies. Sarah King, now Kate Clarke, agreed.

The story about Sarah in the *Kansas City Star* on May 23, 1926, reported that she accompanied her husband on various raids he made on pro-Union towns in Kansas at the end of 1861. William left the Confederate Army five months after the Civil War started because he decided the South was not using the fierce tactics needed to fight as they should. His reputation for hijacking Union mail coaches, attacking Union soldiers, and stealing from them attracted numerous outlaws wanting to join him. Sarah shared a camp with an assortment of brutal men, such as outlaws Jesse and Frank James, and Sam Bass, who traveled by night to keep from being caught by law enforcers. According to the May 5, 1864, *Daily Milwaukee News* in Milwaukee, Wisconsin, she was with William on September 7, 1862, when he and his band attacked and looted Olathe, Kansas, in the dark and early hours of the morning. They quickly fled to an area close to the town of Wellington in Lafayette County, Missouri.

Sarah and William briefly lived in a one-room log cabin near Wellington. One night a lookout spotted federal troops hot on the trail of William's guerrillas, and the pair was forced to abandon their quaint home. Sarah made a getaway with a herd of horses that her husband and his men had stolen. The renegade band met up with her once the coast was clear and regained possession of the fresh mounts. Sarah continued without her husband and took refuge in an area east of Kansas City, Missouri, known as Bone Hill.

In her absence, William's followers grew to more than 400 men. Confederate leaders recognized the powerful influence his raiders had and unofficially commissioned them to defend the Rebel agenda by terrorizing and robbing areas and individuals who sympathized with the North. William's raiders would ride full-gallop into a town, armed with pistols, firing their weapons left and right. Then they would wheel their horses around and be off and away like the wind. They were always able to elude authorities with their hard riding and superior knowledge of the region.

Sarah was hiding out near Fort Scott, Kansas, when on October 17, 1862, her husband and his guerrilla band attacked Shawnee, Kansas. The gang burned the town to the ground and killed a dozen people by shooting them in the backs of their heads.

William and his young bride did not reunite until the end of August 1863. By that time William and his band of outlaws had already viciously attacked Lawrence, Kansas. According to the *Kansas City Star* and the September 1977 *Real West Magazine*, Sarah reported that William "did little other than plan and execute the horrible raid. The by word was "Kill! Kill! Kill! He ordered all males in the town old enough to carry a rifle be destroyed; no women or children were to be harmed." The outcome was much more severe than that. The town's bank and businesses were robbed, 154 buildings belonging to Union sympathizers were ruined, and more than 180 men and boys were slain.

Sarah was waiting for William outside Lawrence after the massacre. In 1926, the *Kansas City Star* reported that "arising before dawn on the morning of the Lawrence massacre, anxious about William's safety, she had left the bushwhacker camp in Missouri and ridden ninety miles in five hours, reaching him, as it turned out, just in time to accompany him on the arduous two-day retreat back across the line. His blood-thirsty group was then disbanded and the couple fled the area and headed to Texas."

The Quantrills spent several weeks camping around Missouri, and it was during this time that he presented her with jewels he had acquired while in Lawrence: seven diamond rings, three pins, and four sets of earrings. By the end of 1863, the couple had returned to the Midwest and established a hideout in the Perche Hills of Howard County, Missouri. Their temporary dwelling in Howard County was "as close to a permanent home the couple ever had," Sarah later told the *Kansas City Star*. William introduced Sarah to a variety of vices there including drinking and smoking. "We whiled away many hours beside the stove, planning the future," she recalled to the *Star*.

William remained in the hills until early 1864. While lying low, the renegade had a chance to organize a new group of guerrilla fighters and plan more attacks on towns that backed the Union's position on the war. Sarah occasionally traveled with her husband and his men, and she later indicated that they always treated her with absolute respect. William and his men trusted Sarah completely. She acted as a lookout for the men, letting them know when Union soldiers were approaching, and helped them strip the dead enemy of any unused ammunition. William and his raiders preferred to have Sarah stitch up their wounds and pull their teeth when needed, rather than a medic they didn't know or could not depend on. In June 1864, William sent Sarah to St. Louis while he returned to Jackson County, Missouri, to rendezvous with some of his old followers. Some of the guerrillas later went with William to Kentucky; others rode into Texas. Among the latter was Jesse James.

Sarah wasn't the only female to reportedly be sent away by William. Sue Mundy, a guerrilla from Tennessee who served with William and his band of fighters, was asked to leave in 1865. According to the *Louisville Journal*, Sue was an artillery specialist with William's group. Her last ride as a guerrilla was in March 1865. The group was headed for Paris, Tennessee, when home guards, loyal to the Union, fired on Mundy and the others, killing one man and injuring another.

Sue and another guerrilla found shelter for their wounded companion in a barn, but word of the skirmish as well as the whereabouts of Sue and the other survivors reached the Union garrison in Louisville. Union troops surrounded the barn, and Sue agreed to surrender after being assured they would be treated as prisoners of war. Three days after their capture Sue was hanged. Once the deceased was buried in an unmarked grave, the truth about Sue was revealed to the public. Sue was, in truth, a man, and his name was Marcellus Jerome Clark. His superiors had nicknamed him "Sue" because of his long hair, and Union officials assumed the twenty-year-old killer was indeed a woman. For a brief period of time, Sarah King and Sue Mundy were two of the most sought after female outlaws connected with William Quantrill.

William's end came after the fight near Smiley, Kentucky, at the Wakefield farm. Sarah was gone by the time he took his last breath and wasn't notified until weeks after his passing that he had left her more than 500 dollars. Sarah used the funds William left her, along with the money she received from the sale of the jewels he had stolen, to set herself up in the boardinghouse business. Authorities found the widow in a small town in southwestern Missouri. Unable to recover the stolen rings and pins William had given her, they decided to let the matter go.

Sarah abandoned the life of a business owner in the late 1860s and returned to Blue Springs, Missouri, to live near her parents. She spent the money she earned from the boardinghouse and its subsequent sale to rebuild her parents' home, which had burned to the ground in an accidental fire.

Sarah married two more times after losing William, and she had one child, Bertha Ivins-Evans. In late 1928, Sarah moved to the Jackson County Home for the Aged to live out the remainder of her days. Most of the residents at the county home said that although Sarah was friendly, she seldom spoke to anyone and mostly kept to herself.

Sarah King died on February 4, 1930. She was laid to rest at the Maple Hill Cemetery in Kansas City, Kansas. She was eighty-two years old. ⟫

CHAPTER SIX

ALICE IVERS

The Gambling Outlaw

T he gamblers at the table in Deadwood, South Dakota, each sized up
the other, showing their best poker faces. This was "Poker Alice's"
gambling house, and she was in her element. She shifted her cigar
to the other corner of her mouth, her attention narrowly focused on the
face of the man holding the only other hand besides hers. All the other
players had folded, tossing their cards onto the table.

"Well, I'll see yah," the man breathed and added another bag of gold
dust to the small mountain of tiny sacks already in the center of the
table. "What yah got, Alice?" he asked.

"You ain't going to raise me again?" Alice said and lifted an eyebrow,
shifting the cigar once more. "No? Well, it's pretty full," she said with a
sweeping gesture displaying her cards. "Three aces and a pair of ladies.
Beat that and the dust is yours."

"Take the pot," her opponent snarled. Disgusted, he rose and
stomped to the door, disappearing into the night.

Alice removed a gun from the folds of her skirt and placed it on the
table in front of her. She considered the possibility that the disgruntled
gambler might walk back into the gaming hall and accuse her of cheat-

ing, and she wanted to be ready. It wouldn't have been the first time Alice Ivers, more famously known as Poker Alice, shot a combative card shark. While working at a gambling parlor in Deadwood in 1890, she successfully fended off a drunken miner who had pulled a knife on a fellow dealer.

Back then, a steady stream of prospectors, ranchers, and cowhands filtered in and out of a Deadwood saloon owned by a man named Bedrock Tom where Alice worked. An inexperienced musician playing an out-of-tune accordion squeezed out a familiar melody, inviting in the pleasure-seekers walking by the establishment. Burlap curtains were pulled over the dusty windows, and fans hung down from the ceiling and turned lazily. A distressed mahogany bar stood along one wall of the business, and behind it was a bartender splashing amber liquid into glasses as fast as he could. A row of tables and chairs occupied the area opposite the bar. Every seat was filled with a card player. Poker Alice sat among a sea of male gamblers. She was alarmingly beautiful, fair-skinned, well-dressed, and slim. She had one eye on the cards she was dealing and another on the men at the game two tables down.

Warren G. Tubbs was studying the cards in his hand so intently he didn't notice the hulk of a man next to him get up and walk around behind him. The huge man with massive shoulders and ham-like hands that hung low at his side peered over Warren's shoulder and eyeballed the mountain of chips before him. Alice's bright-blue eyes carefully watched the brute's actions. She watched as he casually reached for his belt and produced a sharp knife from a leather sheath hanging off his waist. Just as he was about to plunge the weapon into Warren's back, a gunshot rang out.

The frivolity in the saloon came to a sudden halt. A sick look filled the stranger's face, and he slowly dropped the knife. He turned briefly to see from which direction the bullet came. Alice stared back at him, her .38 pistol pointed at his head. The man collapsed face first onto the floor. His body was quickly removed to make way for another player. In a matter of minutes the action inside the tavern returned to normal. Warren caught Alice's gaze and grinned. He nodded to her and waggled his fingers in a kind of salute. She offered a slight smile and turned her attention back to the poker game in front of her.

Historians claim that Alice Ivers was born in Sudbury, Devonshire, England, on February 17, 1853. She came to America when she was three years old. The family settled in the South, where she was graduated from a women's college. Her father was a colonel with the Confederate Army during the Civil War, commanding the Nineteenth Louisiana Infantry. Two of her brothers were killed in the battle of Malvern Hill. Sometime after the close of the war, she married Frank F. Duffield and moved to Leadville, Colorado, where Duffield was killed in a mine explosion.

After her first husband's death, Alice turned to gambling for her livelihood. She married Warren Tubbs, who she thought was a professional gambler—though he soon saw the wisdom of leaving that work to her. She had a reputation for always dealing a fair deck. It was from her steady poker face that she earned her sobriquet. She often boasted that God gave her the best poker face of any man, woman, or child ever made, and seasoned poker players say that a royal flush or a pair of deuces in her hand made no difference in the face of Poker Alice. She gambled for high stakes without a quiver of the hand as she dealt, without the twitch of a face muscle. While playing cards she was a cold as the steel of her .38 revolver.

Alice and Tubbs wandered around the West for more than a year after they were married: Colorado, Nevada, Montana—wherever there was money to be made and men with nerve enough to take on Poker Alice. She broke the bank at faro in Silver City, New Mexico, winning a total of 6,000 dollars. She and her husband continued to travel after that big win.

Alice turned banker and began dealing her own faro game wherever the pair went. She is believed to be the first female faro card dealer in the West, and was very successful. The couple eventually made their way to New York. The purpose for the trip was so Alice could purchase a wardrobe befitting a high-stakes poker player. She bought beautiful gowns, hats, expensive jewelry—all the finery needed to help her gain entrance into the most elite gambling houses west of Independence, Missouri.

Any house would pay twenty-five dollars a week to a female dealer (of which there were few), roughly ten percent more than their male counterparts, but that pay was only a drop in the bucket compared to the thousands Alice made in winnings. According to various newspaper accounts, Alice's exceptional card playing ability was due in large part to the fact that she was a mathematical genius. According to rival gamblers, she had a talent for counting cards and quickly deducing the possible outcome of each hand.

Somewhere during her travels she acquired a taste for alcohol and cigars. When people learned Poker Alice was in town, they would flock to see the talented card player in her extraordinary dresses, puffing on a cigar.

In the winter of 1874, twenty-one-year-old Poker Alice had heard a rumor that there was a sizable amount to be made at the newest boomtown in Colorado called King Solomon's Mine. She went afoot over the Colorado Rockies from Del Norte, on the west side of the San Luis Valley, to King Solomon's Mine. There was no trail, and the snowdrifts were high. Her husband had decided not to make the trip with her. He was a regular at the saloons in Denver and didn't want to be far from a drink at his favorite watering hole. Three eager miners accompanied Alice on the journey. There were only seven people in the mining town on the other end of the trail. By the time Alice built a cabin with her own hands, there were enough miners there for the poker to be hugely profitable. When Alice returned from King Solomon's Mine in 1876, she and Warren followed the gold rush riches to Deadwood, South Dakota. Her reputation preceded her. Residents soon began referring to her as the "Faro Queen of Deadwood." Whenever lawman and gunfighter Wild Bill Hickok was in town, he liked to play against the Queen. In fact, he had invited her to sit in on a hand with him on August 2, 1876, the day Jack McCall shot and killed the legendary Western character. Alice had declined, citing a prior engagement.

In the early 1900s, Warren was suffering with tuberculosis and needed rest. He and Alice purchased a homestead on the Moreau River outside the town of Sturgis, South Dakota, where he could rest and relax. During a blizzard in 1910, Warren developed pneumonia and died. Alice transported his frozen remains in a horse-drawn sled into Sturgis, where his funeral was held and his body was buried. Alice remarried less than a year later. Her new husband was an obnoxious drunk named George Huckert. Huckert died on their third wedding anniversary.

At this point in her long life, Poker Alice rid herself of the fashionable dresses she once wore and took to wearing men's shirts, khaki skirts, and an old campaign hat. Her beauty had all but faded, and her hair had turned silver. The only thing that remained of the Alice of old was her cigars.

In late 1913, Alice bought a profitable "entertainment business"—one that attracted hordes of soldiers stationed at Fort Meade, South Dakota. In addition to female companionship, she also sold bootleg whiskey. A friendly

Alice Ivers, aka Poker Alice of Sturgis. Here she is shown in her later years, smoking a cigar, a vice she became famous for. PHOTO COURTESY OF THE STATE ARCHIVES OF THE SOUTH DAKOTA HISTORICAL SOCIETY

argument there ended in a free-for-all in which a man was killed. Several soldiers had sampled the alcohol served at Poker Alice's establishment, and as the evening wore on they became a bit too unruly in her opinion. A shoving match ensued between two of the enlisted men, and Alice stepped in to stop the fight from escalating further. She fired a rifle in their direction to scare them, but her aim was off. The bullet struck both men, killing one. Police arrested Alice and closed her business. She was charged with murder, but a jury ruled that the shooting was an accident and Alice was acquitted.

Although she was known for the strict rule she had against any crooked games played at her establishment, Alice didn't have much regard for regulations set outside of her place. On more than one occasion she violated the Volstead Act. Named for Andrew Volstead, the Chairman of the House Judiciary Committee, the act prohibited the production, sale, and transport of intoxicating liquors. Poker Alice participated in all three during the years she operated her own business. The second time she was arrested for violating the act, she was pardoned by South Dakota Governor J. W. Bulow.

Poker was Alice's life, and she made no excuses for her line of work or for the trouble she had with the law because of her profession. Her gambling den attracted many unsavory characters who frequently turned violent if they lost. As a result the police were continually called in to restore order.

Though it isn't clear just how much money she won during her lifetime at the game, she always told her children—she had seven children with Warren, but only two survived to adulthood—that she thought her winnings came to more than a quarter of a million dollars.

Alice told the Florence, South Carolina, *Morning News* in 1929 that "the old-time gambling halls did not match the gowns of the women gamblers and the natural splendor of the men. . . . Towns grew too quickly and the demand came too soon." She said, "Sometimes a gambling table was merely set up in the street. The halls were just made of saw logs with a bar at one side, a cleared space for dancing, and the gambling tables at the other end. The setting attracted honest men and outlaws. I proudly admit that at one time or another, I was in both categories."

She explained that dealers worked in shifts. "I generally drew the 12 midnight to 6 A.M. for the miners who didn't get into town till then. This was the hours when guns barked loudly, as frayed nerves sought the gambling

*Attorney Harry Atwater gave Poker Alice her pardon from Governor Bulow
in December 1928 after her second violation of the Volstead Act.*

Poker Alice and six men sit around a gaming table, one man holding a revolver. Pictures of Wild Bill Hickok and Calamity Jane are visible on the wall in the background.
PHOTO COURTESY OF THE STATE ARCHIVES OF THE SOUTH DAKOTA HISTORICAL SOCIETY

dens after hours of grueling physical labor and disappointment when the yellow gold didn't run in the pan. Running home on the streets in the early morning was dangerous, too. Many stray bullets whistled through my hair as I went to and from a shift."

Alice's health began deteriorating after her run-in with the law in 1913. For seventeen years she suffered with one ailment after another. In 1930, the seventy-seven-year-old gambler complained to doctors that she had pain throughout her entire body. They informed her that the problem was her gallbladder and recommended that it be removed. The doctors also told her that the surgery was risky for a woman of her age. Alice, who thrived on risk, decided to go through with the operation.

On February 27, 1930, three weeks after having surgery, Alice passed away. Her estate, which she estimated at one time to be more than a quarter of a million dollars, had been reduced to fifty dollars and a few possessions. Alice is buried in Sturgis at the St. Aloysius Cemetery. ⇒

CHAPTER SEVEN

BELLE BLACK AND JENNIE FREEMAN

Zip Wyatt's Wicked Women

It was almost eight in the morning on June 3, 1894, when Jennie Free-man* and Belle Black rode into the quiet, unassuming town of Fair-view, Oklahoma. The women, who would later be described by the people they robbed as "neither young, fair, nor dashing," steered their mounts toward a large brick building that was a combination mercantile and post office. Although few paid much attention to them, the women smiled politely to passersby going about their daily routines. When Jen-nie and Belle reached the store, they tied their horses to a hitching post and went inside.

A handful of customers browsed through the assortment of mer-chandise on display: blankets, canned goods, fabric, brooms, and knick-knacks. Belle and Jennie did the same. Jennie concentrated on the back of the store and Belle the front. Belle lingered around a long counter near the entrance, inspecting a decorative row of ladies' hats laid across it. She tried on one of the hats, then reached for a nearby hand mirror to check her look. Belle glanced behind the counter and spotted a rifle leaning against a back wall close to the cash register. She caught Jennie's eye as she removed the hat and put it back in place.

Jennie coolly scanned the shelves and barrels in her corner of the store. A pair of six-shooters resting on a table next to several neatly stacked cans of chewing tobacco gave her pause. She gave the weapons a closer look. They were new, unloaded guns with price tags hanging from the barrels.

After several minutes shopping, both women strolled nonchalantly toward the exit. A store clerk called out to them just before they reached the door. "Was there something I could help you ladies find?" the courteous man asked.

"Now that you mention it," Belle said as she stopped and turned around. "That lovely hat on the end," she said, pointing. "How much is it?" The clerk walked over to the item Belle referred to and she followed. The clerk located the price tag tucked inside the brim of the bonnet and showed it to Belle. She studied it for a moment then sadly shook her head. "Thank you for your help," she said as she headed for the exit. She glanced thoughtfully back at the hat one last time before joining Jennie, waiting for her outside.

The two women climbed onto their horses and rode out of town in the same slow, deliberate fashion they arrived. Jennie smiled at Belle and patted the rifle cradled in her lap. The gun was the same one that had been sitting behind the register at the store. Belle's distraction had been effective enough to allow Jennie to steal the weapon.

Five hours later Jennie and Belle returned to Fairview. When they arrived the second time, they were wearing men's clothing and accompanied by outlaw Zip Wyatt and his gang. They helped the desperados rob the mercantile and post office and stole three horses while making their getaway.

According to the *Hutchinson* [Kansas] *News* on August 14, 1895, Jennie and Belle had participated in numerous robberies with Wyatt and his men. The women knew their jobs well. Prior to holding up a post office or a store, the women were supposed to ride to the appointed location to determine how many armed men were on the scene. If they found any unattended guns, they were to take them. Jennie and Belle would then use the weapons in the robbery.

The *Hutchinson News* described Jennie Freeman as a sinister-looking woman, tall and slender with black eyes and thick black hair. Her husband, Matt, briefly became a member of Zip Wyatt's gang in 1891. Nathaniel "Zip" Wyatt was a murderer and a thief from Indiana. He and his fugitive followers were responsible for a variety of crimes committed in Kansas, Illinois, and the

Oklahoma Territory from June 1891 to July 1895. They robbed trains, stole cattle, and killed more than eleven men in the process.

Federal officers arrested Wyatt in July 1891. He escaped from the jail in Guthrie, Oklahoma, on December 31, 1892. A 1,000 dollar reward was offered for Wyatt's capture. A posse was quickly organized to track the desperado, but he managed to elude law enforcement by hiding near the Cimarron River in Major County, Oklahoma. Changing his name to Dick Yeager, Wyatt sought refuge at the home of aspiring outlaw Matt Freeman, who owned a horse ranch in northwest Oklahoma. For more than four months Matt and Jennie provided Wyatt with all the comforts he required; romance soon bloomed between Wyatt and Jennie. Shortly, Wyatt's partner-in-crime Isaac "Ike" Black arrived, along with Black's wife, Belle, and the four abandoned the Freeman home, leaving Matt behind.

Unusual though it was at the time to have women gang members, the ladies proved valuable. After more members were recruited to the gang, plans were made to steal cattle and horses and drive them into Texas to be sold. Jennie and Belle helped the men by carrying messages and supplies to their various camps. An article in the August 14, 1963, edition of the *Guthrie Daily Leader* contained a quote from Marshall Bill Tilghman about the job Jennie and Belle had with the gang:

> "The two women traveled with the team and covered wagon [Wyatt and Black on horseback]," the marshal explained. "They would establish camp near some country post office or store and make some purchases of canned goods or other supplies . . . survey the place thoroughly and note if there were any Winchesters or shotguns setting behind the counter, then go to camp and report to Wyatt and Black who, as soon as night came, would ride to the store, hold up the proprietor and loot the place. . . . They would then ride off in the opposite direction from the camp, make a circuit and go back, hitch up their team and ride behind the wagon as lookouts. Next morning they would be miles away. . . .[There was also a brisk demand for horses for farm power and other uses] and occasionally they would steal a good team, leave the women in camp, and run the horses up the Kansas line and sell them."

The Wyatt-Black gang found a permanent hideout near the head of Salt Creek Canyon in northern Oklahoma. In the canyon was a large cave that had at one time been used by the Dalton gang. According to author and historian Glenn Shirley, the drifting sands of the Salt Plain area in Oklahoma "rapidly obliterated a trail and made it impossible for a posse to follow." The cave had two entrances. The outlaws stayed in the front part of the cave because they could look out and see any enemies approaching from a long distance away. The horses the gang stole were kept in a corral in the back of the cave.

The Wyatt-Black gang robbed logging operations, freight wagons, and settlers traveling through the region. Newspaper accounts of their crimes, as told to reporters by victims, noted that the outlaws consisted of four men and two women. According to the *Wichita Eagle* in Wichita, Kansas, on November 7, 1895, "Belle Black was not a handsome woman by any

Though unusual at the time for gangs to have female members, Belle Black and Jennie Freeman proved to be valuable assets for Zip Wyatt and his gang. The women assisted the men in numerous robberies by surveying the location, reporting back to the gang, then returning dressed as men to participate in the robbery. Belle and Jennie also served as message curriers for the gang before their arrest in 1894. FORT WAYNE SENTINEL

means, yet she is lithe and has a keen eye. . . . Mrs. Freeman is small in stature and quite handsome. She wears her hair short and it curls around the bill of her cap. Both Mrs. Freeman and Mrs. Black led raids on several occasions, and in bravery and daring were not second to any member of the gang."

On November 18, 1893, the Wyatt-Black gang robbed the Hightower Store and Post Office in Arapaho, Oklahoma. On March 28, 1894, they robbed the general store and post office in Blaine County, Oklahoma. Edward Townsend, the owner of the store, was shot and killed in the holdup. One of the murderers was tracked to his relatives' home in Logan County, Oklahoma. The marshal in charge of the arrest tried to persuade him to tell police where Wyatt, Black, and the other gang members were hiding, but he refused. The shooter was tried, convicted, and sentenced to life in jail.

In spite of the loss of one of their members, the Wyatt-Black gang continued on with their nefarious ways. Throughout April and May 1894, Jennie and Belle helped Wyatt and Black steal pension funds and livestock from farmers throughout northern Oklahoma. The outlaw women were finally apprehended for their misdeeds on June 4, 1894, by law enforcement agents who followed them to their cave hideout. According to the *Kingfisher Free Press* in Oklahoma, on June 27, 1895, "Belle Black and Jennie Freeman were captured as they attempted to escape from a dugout near the cave where the outlaws quartered . . . and when searched they had in their possession money and valuables taken from the [Fairview] post office."

Zip Wyatt and Ike Black managed to escape the June 1894 raid on their hideout, but they were injured in the process. Wyatt was shot through the left arm and Black was shot in the right heel.

In late October 1894, Jennie and Belle were taken to Alva, Oklahoma, to appear before a grand jury. The November 7, 1894, *Alva Republic* reported that "after a thorough examination, the women were discharged without indictment." The newspaper noted that the jury found no evidence of "a criminal nature against the women, other than the fact that they were present with the two outlaws."

Given the rarity of women outlaws at the time, newspapers and dime novels carried story after story about the lady renegades and the lives they lived. Prior to Belle and Jennie being released from the jail in Alva, Oklahoma, the women were the center of attraction for many visitors. "Unlike the female bandits of romance books, these female outlaws had their own manner of dress," the August 14, 1895, edition of the *Hutchinson News* noted. "Instead of being dressed in the dashing cowboy garb, they wore the attire usual of the wives and farmers and working men, save that one wore boots and spurs to aid her in urging her horse when attempting to outride the deputy marshals."

On May 30, 1896, the *Fort Wayne Sentinel* reported that Belle Black and Jennie Freeman were

> . . . victims of circumstances over which they had no control. The capture of the female bandits dispelled the popular myth of the lady bandit. "Neither woman has the appearance of a desperate criminal. Mrs. Freeman, who eloped from her husband with the leader of the gang has defied sheriffs and has robbed right and left. It was not known that Mrs. Freeman or Mrs. Black were women during the raids because the two women always dressed like men.
>
> Mrs. Black and her husband came to western Kansas six years ago and were financially embarrassed through failure of crops. They took to stealing cattle and were obliged to hide to escape arrest. A gang of desperadoes gradually joined them. Zip Wyatt, the leader, was a cowboy who came to Guthrie once a month to spend his wages in high living and it was here that he met Mrs. Freeman, who was an Illinois girl who had formed an incorrect idea of the glories of a bandit's life from too many trashy novels. He persuaded her to elope with him after he had killed two or three men and gone into hiding. He has often puzzled the sheriff as they have fired their rifles at him point blank, and he has escaped without injury.
>
> Since her capture, Mrs. Freeman says Wyatt always wears steel plates over his back, front and thighs and will never be taken alive.

On August 1, 1895, Zip Wyatt and Ike Black were overtaken by a posse four miles outside of the town of Cantonment, Oklahoma. Black was shot in the head and killed. Wyatt was captured after being shot in the chest by lawmen. Before dying of his wounds at the jail in Enid, Oklahoma, on September 7, 1895, he admitted to killing eleven men.

According to the story as told by Marshal Bill Tilghman that later appeared in the *Guthrie Daily Leader* on August 14, 1963, Jennie Freeman became an evangelist and preached throughout the same section of country where she rode and scouted with the Wyatt-Black gang. Belle Black moved to Missouri where she married a successful farmer. Belle and her husband had three children, and she became a respected member of the community. ⟞

Although their names were spelled the same and their criminal actions took place around the same time, Jennie Freeman, the outlaw who ran with Zip Wyatt's gang, and Jennie Freeman, the "Railroad Fakir" (see Chapter 4) are two different, unrelated people.

CHAPTER EIGHT

VICTORIA WOODHULL
The Obscene Outlaw

O hio native Victoria Claflin Woodhull was one of the most controversial outlaws in the Midwest. Her arrest in early November 1872 on federal obscenity charges attracted the attention of political pundits and social reformers from Washington, D.C., to the Wyoming Territory. The press called her "a most immoral woman," and hundreds of newspaper reporters were on hand the day Victoria was arrested in New York, hoping to capture a sensationalized statement from the outspoken outlaw.

New York marshals brought thirty-four-year-old Victoria and her twenty-seven-year-old sister, Tennessee Claflin, to court on Saturday, November 2, 1872. Word that the attractive suffragettes were going to appear before a judge spread quickly. By the time the two women arrived at the courthouse in Manhattan, the horde of excited journalists flitted around them like water bugs. The accused sisters were both dressed in black taffeta. Victoria's expression was serious. Tennessee's look was less somber, and according to newspaper reporters covering the story, she gave the journalists and onlookers at the scene an approving smile.

The Claflin sisters had dared to publish their own newspaper, called the *Woodhull & Claflin's Weekly*, and print scandalous ideas advocating "free love." In a letter Victoria sent to the *New York Times* in 1871, she claimed that free love was the "only cure for immorality, the deep damnation by which men corrupt and disfigure God's most holy institution of sexual relations." She goes on, "It is not marriage but sexual intercourse, then, that is God's most holy institution." Victoria and Tennessee's progressive views on sex and the brazen printing of those ideals appalled citizens not only in the United States but in other countries like Germany and Russia as well. They "threaten to destroy the morals nations so desperately needed to cling to," was the opinion voiced in the *New York Times* on November 23, 1871.

Victoria and Tennessee were not strangers to confrontation with the law. Their father, Reuben Buckman "Buck" Claflin, was a scoundrel who excelled at breaking the rules of conventional society and spent time behind bars for his actions. Buck and his wife, Roxanna Hummel, lived in a rundown house in Homer, Ohio. The couple had ten children. Born on September 23, 1838, Victoria was the Claflins' sixth child. Although Victoria's father claimed to be a lawyer with his own profitable practice, he was actually a skilled thief with no law degree at all. He owned and operated a gristmill and also worked as a postmaster. Buck supplemented his income by stealing from merchants and business owners, and he was a counterfeiter and a suspected arsonist.

Victoria's mother was a religious fanatic who dismissed Buck's illegal activities in favor of chastising her neighbors for what she claimed was hedonism. Her public prayers were loud, judgmental, and dramatic. She preached to her children and insisted they memorize long passages of the Old Testament. By the time Victoria was eight, she was able to recite the Bible from cover to cover. Reflecting on her life, Victoria wrote in *Autobiography of Victoria Claflin* that her mother's spiritual zeal so influenced her childhood that young Victoria believed she could see into the future and predict what was to come of those who sought her out to preach.

Tennessee was reported to be the true clairvoyant of the family. Born in 1845, she was the last child born to Roxanna and Buck. Roxanna claimed Tennessee had the power to perceive things not present to the senses. She would slip into trances and speak with spirits, answering voices no one else could hear.

Victoria and Tennessee had very little formal education. Although Victoria attended school for only four years, she was bright, precocious, and well

Victoria Woodhull. SPECIAL COLLECTIONS, VASSAR COLLEGE LIBRARIES

read. She was uninhibited and at the age of eleven delivered sermons from a busy spot in Homer. When she wasn't regaling an audience with biblical tales, she was boasting of her ability to remember back to the day she was born. "When I first saw the light of day on this planet," she said, "it seemed I had been rudely awakened from a death-like sleep. How well I remember the conversation between the doctor and my father as they handed me over to the nurse. I remember looking back at my mother's face at that moment, the look of pain and anguish burnt into my plastic brain, and often during my young babyhood I would watch as she suckled me."

The Claflins left Homer under a cloud of controversy in 1849. The gristmill Buck owned burned to the ground under suspicious circumstances. The mill was losing money, and Buck frequently mentioned to townspeople that he was desperate to get rid of the business. Residents believed that Buck set fire to the mill in order to collect a 500 dollar insurance payout on the property. After collecting, Buck quickly left town, soon followed by Roxanna and the children.

Not long after they arrived in Mount Gilead, Ohio, Buck found a new scheme. He trotted out his daughters Victoria and Tennessee, announcing the girls' talents for "second sight" or "extrasensory perception," which is the ability to receive information in the form of a vision, and channeling spirits. Buck rented a theater and charged patrons seventy-five cents to watch the four-year-old and eleven-year-old communicate with deceased Claflin family members and predict the future, specifically that one day a woman would be president of the United States.

As an adult, Victoria explained her abilities to reporters at the *Anglo-American* newspaper in 1871:

> My spiritual vision dates back as early as my third year. In my hometown of Homer, Ohio, a young woman named Rachel Scribner, who had been my nurse and was about twenty-five years of age, suddenly died. On the day of her death I was picked up by her departing spirit and borne off into the spirit world. I felt myself gliding through the air like St. Catharine winged away by angels. My mother tells me that while this scene was enacting to my inner consciousness, my body lay as if dead for three hours. My chief

guardian in the spirit world is a matured man of stately figure, clad in a Greek tunic, solemn and graceful, strong in influence and altogether dominant over my life. He will not tell me his name—he only promises that in due time I will know his identity. Meanwhile he prophesied to me that I would rise to great distinction; that I would emerge from poverty and live in a stately house; that I would win great wealth in a city which he pictured as crowded; that I would publish and conduct a journal; and that finally, to crown my career, become the ruler of my people.

Victoria and Tennessee's shows, in which they would conduct séances and interpret dreams for audience members, attracted a large following, and in a short time the two young girls became the sole source of income for their family.

At the age of fifteen, Victoria married a twenty-eight-year-old doctor named Canning Woodhull. The doctor had moved to Mount Gilead from Rochester, New York, to set up a practice. The pair met when Victoria's parents asked Canning to treat Victoria when she was suffering from rheumatism and a fever. Five months after nursing his patient back to health, the two were married. They exchanged vows on November 20, 1853. Canning was possessive and demanding, and Victoria grew to dislike being under the rule of a husband. He had also misrepresented himself. Canning told Victoria his father was a judge and that he had a close friendship with the mayor of the city. Not only did the teenage bride eventually learn her father-in-law was not a judge, but she discovered that the family had no political connections at all. What's more, Victoria found out that Canning had no medical training and was an alcoholic. With Canning unable to support the couple financially, Victoria was forced to return to the stage to perform her séances and dream interpretations.

In December 1854, she gave birth to her first child, a son she named Byron. The baby was born with Down's syndrome, and Victoria was heartbroken. She blamed her husband's drinking for the boy's condition. She believed alcohol had a debilitating effect on health and that those issues were passed on to Byron. Canning's alcoholism and womanizing, combined with the strain of raising a child with special needs, caused even more problems between Victoria and her husband. Hoping that a change of scenery might improve their marital condition, Victoria made arrangements to move her family to California. By the fall of 1855, the Woodhulls were living in the bustling gold rush city of San Francisco.

The new setting did not change Victoria's situation. Her husband continued to drink and refused to find steady employment. With her baby in tow, Victoria found odd jobs including selling cigars and working as a seamstress. Three years after the Woodhulls moved to San Francisco, Victoria claimed to have received a vision of her sister Tennessee calling for her to return home. According to Theodore Tilton, editor of the newspaper *The Independent* and Claflin family biographer, Victoria wasted no time packing her family's things, boarding a steamship, and traveling back to Ohio.

Buck Claflin had made arrangements for his daughters to perform their supernatural abilities at a theater in Columbus, Ohio. He instructed the women to listen closely to individual audience members' requests and then encourage them to give large sums of money to the sisters to heal minor ailments or serious diseases or to predict the outcome of a future event. There is no evidence to suggest that Victoria had any problems with defrauding members of the audience. In 1859, the sister act of Woodhull and Claflin earned more than 100,000 dollars.

Victoria and Tennessee toured most of the Midwest's big cities, and their traveling medicine show attracted the attention not only of the frail and desperate but of law enforcement as well. Authorities were concerned that the sisters were charlatans and would have to be stopped. "The sisters were superbly equipped for a career in the shadowy realm that lies between complete [integrity] and outright crime," noted a feature on the sisters in the *Oakland Tribune* on March 9, 1964. "They peddled a magic elixir . . . with Tennessee's picture on the bottle. They were making a nice living."

The Woodhulls' marriage continued to be mired in mistrust, due in large part to Canning's infidelities and continued drinking. Victoria prayed for another child, with the hope that it would help improve her relationship with her husband. In the spring of 1861, Zula Maude was born. Much to Victoria's relief the infant was healthy.

According to Zula's own memoirs, her mother "brought all her faculties to bear on me while carrying me that I should not be like Byron." Victoria and Canning doted on their daughter, but the baby could not repair the damage in the relationship. Historian Herb Michelson believed the cause of Canning's infidelity and alcoholism was Victoria, who blamed him for Byron's health problems. In the feature in the *Oakland Tribune* in 1964, Michelson noted that "Victoria brought Woodhull untold misery for the role she believed he played in their child's handicap and he became a human derelict as a result." The Woodhulls separated in 1864.

The demise of Victoria's marriage did not distract her from her work. She continued to mesmerize audiences with her so-called powers of mystical observation. While her divorce was being finalized, Victoria appeared on stage without Tennessee. Buck realized he could double the family income if he divided the act in two. He booked the women in different theaters, and, as predicted, their earnings were twice as large.

In June 1864, however, a run-in with the law threatened to bring an end to performances by Woodhull and Claflin and bankrupt the family. At a show in Pittsburgh, Pennsylvania, Tennessee laid hands on an audience member suffering from cancer and told the woman she had healed her. The ailing woman died a few weeks after the program, and authorities announced plans to charge Tennessee with manslaughter. The family fled before an arrest could be made.

Victoria and Tennessee then traveled to Cincinnati, Ohio. It was there that Victoria persuaded her sister to let her manage their careers instead of their father. Tennessee agreed. Buck was annoyed but accepted the decision and returned to the rest of his family in Ohio. The attractive sister act took to the stage, again showing off their clairvoyant abilities, this time also promoting a tonic that promised to cure any ailment and lift the spirits. Law enforcement officers responded to complaints that the tonic was more alcohol than medicine. Accusations were also made that Victoria and Tennessee were running a brothel, and that they were adulteresses and blackmailers—claims Victoria vehemently denied. According to the September 30, 1871, *Anglo-American Times*, Victoria reported that the allegations were made by "skeptical women whose husbands frequented Woodhull and Claflin performances." Hoping to shake the rumors that plagued them in Cincinnati, Victoria and her sister made their way to Chicago. Within a month of arriving in Illinois, Victoria was in trouble with the law again, this time for fraudulent fortune-telling.

Victoria fled south to Tennessee with her sister, and, in late 1864, the pair joined a traveling medicine show her father had organized. The freight wagon carrying Victoria and her children, parents, and siblings stopped at small towns ravaged by the Civil War. Woodhull and Claflin preyed on families dealing with the devastating loss of loved ones. Promising to rid communities of diseases such as cancer, cholera, and diphtheria, Victoria and Tennessee laid their hands on the sick and frail, recited mysterious incantations, and sent them on their way. The sisters made the ailing believe their illnesses would be gone in twenty-four hours. By the time their promises proved empty, the supposed healers were long gone.

In April 1865, the medicine show rolled into St. Louis, Missouri. Tired of living and working out of a wagon, Victoria rented a hotel suite for herself and her two children. Many people seeking to speak with their sons, brothers, and husbands who had been killed in the Civil War called on Victoria for help. Colonel James H. Blood, commander of the 6th Army and St. Louis' newly elected city auditor, was one of many people who visited Victoria at her suite. He needed Victoria's spiritual counsel on a matter regarding his future. James was in an unhappy marriage and wanted to know if he should leave his wife.

Victoria and James were instantly drawn to each other. She said nothing about the attraction she felt for him and attended to the business at hand. She passed into a trance and perceived that his future destiny was to be linked with hers in marriage. When Victoria came out of the trance, she told James what she had seen. As both took such visions seriously, they pledged themselves to one another. "We were married by the powers in the air at that moment," James later wrote in his memoirs.

Victoria and James began having an affair almost immediately after they met. Victoria believed a sexual relationship connected individuals not only physically but also spiritually. Much to the dismay of those who held to conventional standards that sex should be limited to the confines of marriage, Victoria openly expressed the joy derived from sexual encounters outside the institution. Her progressive opinion brought criticism from so-called polite society and speculation that she engaged in prostitution. James was captivated by Victoria's unorthodox views. She abandoned her family and children and ran off with James to Dayton, Ohio. James divorced his wife and married Victoria on July 15, 1866.

After the wedding ceremony, Mr. and Mrs. Blood went to New York. Victoria held public healings and séances in New York City and James joined her in her work. He took copious notes documenting the various spirits she channeled and the instruction they offered during midnight sessions his wife had with paid audience members. "Victoria and I regarded all the other portions of our lives as almost valueless compared to these times," James was quoted in the *Anglo-American Times*.

When Victoria wasn't on stage, she was discussing her "free-love" theory with like-minded people who felt women should not only be able to act on their sexual impulses but also that they should run for public office. According to Victoria's autobiography, it was a goal she had long pondered. At the time, laws prohibited women from voting, but not from running for office. Victoria noted in her memoirs that the majority of men did not view any woman running for office as a real threat. As she saw it, her political aspirations would gain her a larger audience for her fortune-telling business.

By 1867, Victoria's parents, siblings, and children made their way to New York. In December of that year, Victoria said her "guardian" came to her in a dream and shared a prediction that promised to be beneficial to her and her family. According to the September 30, 1871, edition of the *Anglo-American Times*, her guardian communicated a message to Victoria on a scroll. The document, which came to be known as "The Memorial of Victoria C. Woodhull," was a petition addressed to Congress. The document claimed the right of women to vote, under the Fourteenth Amendment, in "the States wherein they reside." It noted that "the State of New York, of which she was a citizen, should be restrained by Federal authority from preventing her exercise of this constitutional right."

Buck believed the idea revealed to his daughter was indeed delivered by a spiritual guardian—and that the document could prove profitable, given the controversial nature of its contents. Victoria and Tennessee, who firmly believed women should have the right to vote, were in favor of their father's idea to launch a new show and take the message of women's right to vote to the masses, but they lacked capital to launch the endeavor. Buck quickly found a financial supporter in Cornelius Vanderbilt. The seventy-three-year-old multi-millionaire frequently consulted spiritualists to attempt to communicate with his deceased parents and wife. In exchange for an investment in this new venture, Buck promised that his daughters would be Vanderbilt's personal on-call spiritualists. Vanderbilt enthusiastically agreed.

Victoria's time with the wealthy man was spent predicting stock market trends, "looking into the future" and advising him on what to buy and sell. Tennessee was tasked with healing his arthritis and rheumatism.

Vanderbilt found the women bewitching. He grew quite fond of the sisters and trusted them implicitly. The sisters abandoned their spiritualist shows and devoted all their time to Vanderbilt. In return he helped the women grow their own stock portfolio, and, with the financial freedom she realized from Vanderbilt's tutelage, Victoria began pursuing her goal to secure women's right to vote. Other women such as Elizabeth Cady Stanton and Harriet Beecher Stowe had the same objective in mind, but Victoria's preoccupation with spiritualism and following the directive of a guardian in the hereafter distracted from the importance of the message. As a result the most influential leaders in the movement kept their distance from her.

The stock market crashed in 1869, but Victoria, Tennessee, and Vanderbilt survived the disaster with their fortunes intact, even increasing their wealth. They had purchased large quantities of gold in anticipation that the price would go up. Their gamble paid off. Vanderbilt helped Victoria and Tennessee establish a brokerage firm. On February 5, 1870, the sisters became the first female Wall Street brokers. Wall Street veterans were shocked at the sight of women peddling stocks and were more than a little skeptical that they would be successful. When word leaked to the market that Victoria and her sister's firm Woodhull, Claflin & Company was backed by Vanderbilt, it got the attention of a large number of investors looking for a place to put their money. In three weeks the ladies reportedly made 700,000 dollars.

The ladies' popularity grew as a result of their financial accomplishments. They also attracted the attention of law enforcement officials from jurisdictions where the women had prior legal trouble. When confronted by the police about the charges of fraudulent fortune-telling pending against them in Chicago and Pennsylvania, Tennessee claimed she wasn't the woman they wanted. The authorities didn't believe her. Both Tennessee and Victoria were charged and bound over for trial. Both women lost their court cases and paid substantial fines.

Victoria worked hard to repair the damage the negative publicity caused their firm and her political ambitions. She persuaded civil rights leader Susan B. Anthony to write an article about the stockbrokerage firm operated by her and her sister, both now known as "the Queens of Finance." The article complimented the sisters' gifts for making money but was not as generous in referring to their practice of spiritualism. According to Victoria Woodhull's biography, written by Mary Gabriel, she wanted to be accepted by Anthony and her followers fighting to gain women's right to vote but doubted she'd ever be able to fully secure their approval. She believed she had something to offer the cause and was compelled to make a difference.

In April 1870, Victoria Claflin Woodhull Blood declared herself a candidate for president of the United States. The idea to run for president against Ulysses Simpson Grant was Victoria's alone and was fueled by her desire to reform the national political arena through uniform wages, public works programs, and direct taxation. While mapping out her platform, she and her sister decided to branch out into another area of business. Using funds provided by Vanderbilt, Victoria started a newspaper, calling it *Woodhull & Claflin's Weekly*. They published the first issue of the paper on May 14, 1870. The front page stated the periodical's mission: "This journal will be primarily devoted to the vital interests of people and will treat all matters freely and without reservation. It will support Victoria C. Woodhull for President, with its whole strength. With one Victoria on the throne of England and another as president of the U.S. there will be a sisterhood of Victorias."

While Victoria divided her time between campaigning for the highest office in the land, working at the brokerage firm, and writing for *Woodhull & Claflin's Weekly*, Tennessee was working on other ways the newspaper could benefit her and her sister. The sisters had schemed themselves into the upper strata of political leaders and lawmakers, and they learned quickly they could blackmail those individuals by promising to keep their private lives out of the paper. Some believe it was because of such tactics that Victoria was granted the opportunity to speak before the House Judiciary Committee on women's suffrage at the National Woman Suffrage Association convention in January 1871.

If Victoria had limited her speech to making a case for women's constitutional freedoms listed in the Fourteenth and Fifteenth Amendments—

Victoria argued for women's suffrage in front of the Judiciary Committee of the House of Representatives on the basis of the Fourteenth and Fifteenth Constitutional Amendments, as depicted in this drawing from an 1871 edition of Frank Leslie's Illustrated Newspaper. LIBRARY OF CONGRESS, PRINTS AND PHOTOGRAPHS DIVISION LC-USZ62-2023

giving voting rights to all citizens—then perhaps leaders such as Elizabeth Cady Stanton, Isabella Beecher Hooker, and Susan B. Anthony would have supported her political aspirations. Instead she talked about the benefits of free love, and many convention organizers and attendees felt the concept was too radical and potentially dangerous. Traditional suffragettes believed free love was a threat to the sanctity of marriage and families. If women had the freedom to have sex with anyone other than their spouses, they questioned who would take care of the children that might be conceived. The idea that sexually transmitted diseases would spread rapidly with such promiscuity was also an issue.

Harriet Beecher Stowe and her sister Catharine Beecher made their displeasure with Victoria's view evident in the books they wrote. In Harriet's book entitled *My Wife and I*, she referred to Victoria as "a brainless free lover who spoke of women's rights without knowing what they were." Catharine Beecher warned Victoria that she would make life difficult for her if she continued speaking about free love. Victoria would not be intimidated.

The articles that appeared in *Woodhull & Claflin's Weekly* were just as contentious as Victoria's public addresses. What began as a somewhat tame women's rights publication soon turned into a tabloid-style periodical filled with sex and vice. The weekly featured reports of corruption in local and national government, general gossip about some of the country's most elite, how-to divorce tips, directions on how to perform an abortion, and articles about prostitution, how to operate a brothel, and women's rights. Critics like author Harriet Beecher Stowe, civil rights leader Susan B. Anthony, and the editorial staff at *Harper's Weekly* spoke out against the topics covered in the paper, and rumor spread that Victoria was "not only amoral but a repeat criminal offender with nothing but legal woes on the horizon." Victoria and Tennessee were referred to as "jezebels" and accused of being "disreputable business women who were addicted to drugs and slept with other women's husbands." A series of past lawsuits proved that last piece of gossip to be true. Adultery was against the law in most states.

In February 1871, the sisters were sued for misappropriating money from their stockbrokerage clients. A court found the women guilty of embezzlement. Within a few weeks of the court's decision, Henry Ward Beecher, minister and publisher of the newspaper the *Christian Union*, alleged that *Woodhull & Claflin's Weekly* was printing libels. Beecher offered no specifics, however. The embezzlement convictions and libel allegation devastated Victoria's personal and professional life. Zula Maude, her daughter, who was now twelve years old, had to change schools and take a different name to keep from being harassed. Victoria and James argued over the continuation of her political involvement. The family struggled financially, and, in early 1872, Victoria and Tennessee were forced to suspend publishing the newspaper for a short period of time.

Victoria tried to rise above the various setbacks and pressed forward with her run for the presidency. On May 10, 1872, she was the keynote speaker at the convention for her political party, the Equal Rights Party. She was officially nominated for president of the United States, and Frederick Douglass was her running mate (though he was not asked and never consented to the notion). *Woodhull & Claflin's Weekly* was up and running again after the nomination was made.

"GET THEE BEHIND ME, (MRS.) SATAN!"—[SEE PAGE 165.]

WIFE (with heavy burden). "I'D RATHER TRAVEL THE HARDEST PATH OF MATRIMONY THAN FOLLOW YOUR FOOTSTEPS."

Victoria Woodhull was vilified for her comments about "free love." Many women, as depicted in this drawing, referred to Woodhull as Mrs. Satan. This drawing appeared in Harper's Weekly *in 1872.* LIBRARY OF CONGRESS, PRINTS AND PHOTOGRAPHS DIVISION LC-USZ62-74994

In retaliation for the negative attention she had received (primarily from the Beecher family), Victoria ran a story in September 1872 about an affair Reverend Henry Ward Beecher was rumored to be having with a member of his congregation. In addition to the exposé about Beecher, the *Weekly* featured an article about a corrupt stockbroker named Luther Challis. According to information Tennessee offered to the paper, Challis frequently boasted about seducing young girls. He bragged that he would "ply them with alcohol first then have sex with them." The *Weekly* noted that Challis claimed "the bloody proof of the loss of one girl's virginity on his fingers." The scandalous issue of the newspaper was sent to 5,000 subscribers via the U.S. Postal Service.

On November 2, 1872, an agent of the Society for the Suppression of Obscene Literature appeared before the United States Commissioner asking for the arrest of Victoria Woodhull and Tennessee Claflin. Five days later, Iowa's *Monticello Express* reported that the agent's request was promptly granted. "The sisters were arrested at their brokerage firm and driven to the United States Marshal's office," the article noted. Victoria and Tennessee were subsequently charged with circulating obscene and indecent publications through the mail, the penalty for which, as prescribed by statute, was imprisonment for one year and a fine of 500 dollars. Three thousand copies of the newspaper containing the alleged obscene matter were confiscated from the sisters' business.

The bail set for the "Obscene Outlaws," as the press called them, was 3,000 dollars each. The *Monticello Express* also reported that Colonel Blood was arrested for complicity in the alleged slanderous publication. He persisted in declaring that he knew nothing about the matter, but a grand jury did not believe him. His bail was set at 1,500 dollars. Victoria and Tennessee's trial began on November 7, 1872, and continued through the beginning of December. According to the *Anglo-American Times* on November 23, 1872, the women denied that they did anything wrong. The *Times'* report pointed out that few people agreed with them, and many felt their behavior set the women's rights movement back. "It is shown that the rise of these two wretched creatures into notoriety grows out of the new doctrine [of women's rights], that it makes no difference for the purpose of a movement what a woman's character is, provided she is sound on the main question," the article noted.

"When the well-established canons of human experience as to the value of female modesty have been cast to the winds, this dismal result follows."

The initial criminal case against the sisters was eventually dismissed, but misdemeanor charges were upheld. The women paid a half million dollars in fines and bail; the government confiscated their printing press, personal papers, and their brokerage firm. From November 1872 to June 1873, Victoria and Tennessee were arrested seven more times on similar obscenity and libel charges. They were acquitted each time they went to court because the jury couldn't reach a decision. The cost of paying for so many attorneys led to the sisters' bankruptcy, the eventual collapse of *Woodhull & Claflin's Weekly*, and the demise of Victoria's political aspirations. With no funds to invest in another run for the White House and no real hope of persuading the public at large to vote for a woman, Victoria's political party was dissolved. She believed she had made great strides for womanhood, but critics felt she'd only made a mockery of the presidential process.

Colonel Blood and Victoria divorced in 1878, and she married British banker John Biddulph Martin in 1883. The couple moved to England shortly after they wed. Victoria died at her home in North Park, England, on June 9, 1927, when she was eighty-eight years old. Tennessee preceded her sister in death. The two had been estranged for years after they were forced out of the publishing business. Tennessee died in England on January 18, 1923, at the home of one of her nieces. She was seventy-seven years old. ⇥

CHAPTER NINE

ANNE COOK

Lincoln County Outlaw

T hose who knew Anne Cook called her cruel, unfeeling, and motivated by money. The brothel she operated in North Platte, Nebraska, in the early 1900s was a profitable enterprise, but she wanted to amass a fortune, and one house of ill-repute was not enough. According to those who knew the Cook family well, Anne's teenage daughter, Clara, brought in a substantial amount of income working for her at the brothel. Clients requested the thirteen-year-old on a regular basis.

By the time Clara was in her thirties, she had fully adopted her mother's quest for wealth. In addition to entertaining callers, Clara was the bookkeeper for Anne's various illegal enterprises. Among Anne's nefarious business ventures were bootlegging, gambling, and extortion. In turn, Clara used what she knew about her mother's criminal behavior to extort money from Anne and enlarge her own bank account. The pair often fought over the misappropriation of funds. Clara misjudged how far Anne would go to maintain the property, money, and power she had acquired.

On May 29, 1934, then forty-year-old Clara challenged her mother for the last time. Family members at the sprawling farm where they lived in Lincoln County, Nebraska, told authorities that the pair had been arguing most of the day. No one was certain of the nature of the quarrel—only that Anne had settled the heated discussion by killing her daughter.

The fight began in the kitchen. At some point Clara stormed out of the house, and Anne followed after her with a cast-iron bar used to lift the lids off the stove. Anne's sister, Elizabeth "Liz" Peete, saw her throw the bar and hit Clara in the head. Clara didn't fall down immediately, but when she did the right side of her head was bleeding profusely. Liz later told a reporter that Anne stood in stunned silence for a moment, staring at the dark liquid covering the ground under her daughter's mass of auburn hair. Anne went inside the house and grabbed a towel to wrap around her daughter's head. After she had completed the gruesome task, she coolly walked back into the parlor of the house and called the family physician.

Shortly after the doctor arrived, he pronounced Clara dead. Anne was informed that her daughter's body needed to be transported to town to be embalmed. Contemplating the questions that might arise, she resisted the idea at first. After deciding that no one would dare inquire as to what happened, Anne agreed to let the ambulance take her daughter away.

While Clara's father and the doctor talked over the details of transporting the deceased, Anne ordered her adopted son, twenty-one-year-old Joe, to her side. In a hushed but stern voice, she ordered Joe to retrieve a bag of money Clara had hidden away in her closet. She told him to move the money to the cellar until the matter with Clara was settled.

Anne insisted Clara's death was an accident, and the county coroner, J. Matthews, deemed an inquest was not necessary. His initial examination showed that blunt force trauma was the cause of death. On May 30, 1934, the *North Platte Bulletin* in Nebraska reported that an anonymous witness had come forward suggesting that Clara's death was not accidental—and was not the result of just a head injury. The witness told authorities that Anne had instructed one of the boarders who lived at the farm to prepare a dose of poison she could slip into her daughter's food. Anne denied the accusation. Through broken sobs she explained how the boarder accidentally poured the lethal concoction into a glass that Clara then unwittingly drank from. The newspaper article explained that the young woman did not die solely from a blow to the head, but from poison that entered her lungs and suffocated her.

Investigators could not adequately prove Clara's death was intentional—much to the dismay of the Lincoln County residents who disliked Anne and suspected she was guilty of many more crimes in addition to the murder of her daughter. Clara was laid to rest at the North Platte cemetery. According to an interview with Joe for the biography about Anne Cook by Nellie Snyder Yost, *Evil Obsession*, mere hours after the funeral, Anne sent Joe to the cellar for Clara's money sack. The funds were quickly added to Anne's stash of cash that she kept in a secret location at the Cook farm.

The woman whose extraordinary greed drove her to the most heartless of crimes was born Anna M. Peete on July 15, 1873, in Denver, Colorado. Her parents were ranchers and owned a big house with stables. They were well respected in the community of Nunn, Colorado, and all their investments were profitable. They had five children: two girls and three boys. The

Born in February 1894, Clara Cook was physically and verbally abused by her mother Anne, who saw her as a source of labor to generate income. Clara, however, became as ruthless as her mother and extorted money from Anne. On May 29, 1934, the two argued for the last time. The fight would leave Clara dead, killed by a blow from a cast-iron bar thrown by her mother. COURTESY OF VICTOR RAMIREZ

oldest son married young and worked with his father. The two other Peete boys became ministers. Anne grew up and married Frank Cook, and together they raised corn and wheat on a farm in Hershey, Nebraska. Anne's younger sister, Elizabeth, seemed to be the only child that lacked direction.

According to Joe's recollections about his great-grandparents and stories Anne told him, Elizabeth seemed disinterested in men and unmotivated to do anything outside the home. In 1898, Anne's parents asked if Liz could move in with her. They hoped Liz might find her place in life if she spent some time with her older sister. Anne agreed—but not out of any true sense of loyalty to Liz. She saw her sister as a source of labor around the farm. And she knew Liz would some day be given their parents' home and some of their savings when they died. Anne set her sights on Liz's inheritance.

Anne seldom if ever considered her husband Frank when making decisions about their homestead. The two had married in 1891, and Anne recognized from the start that Frank was not as ambitious as she required. He was content to own and work the few acres he cultivated, but Anne had bigger plans. After ten years of marriage, she had expanded their property holdings on either side of the farmhouse and added poultry and livestock, an apple orchard, and cherry trees to their business ventures. Frank took out a mortgage to fund some of the growth, but it was Anne's side jobs that provided the bulk of the financing.

Professing to suffer from back and kidney problems, Anne made frequent trips to Omaha to meet with a doctor. In truth, she was entertaining customers at a brothel that employed her services. According to Nellie Snyder Yost's book *Evil Obsession*, Anne liked her job at the brothel; considering the money she made, she was quite good at it.

The Cooks became parents in February 1894. As soon as Clara was old enough, Anne put her to work on the farm. She did the same with Liz's daughter, Mary, born in July 1902. Liz had met and married Joe Knox, a cowboy from the Sandhills ranch country near Hyannis, Nebraska. The relationship was conducted in secret, and when Anne found out she was furious. She viewed Liz as her property—a necessity to keep the farm running. In 1905 Anne invited Liz and Mary to visit, and immediately put them to work. She then intercepted letters between Liz and her husband, cutting off all communication. Twice Joe tried to rescue his wife and child, but both times

Anne ran him off the property with a shotgun. Joe then asked law enforcement to help him, but Anne had paid them a sizable sum to stay away. Joe eventually gave up and filed for divorce.

Anne physically and verbally abused her daughter Clara, as well as Liz and Mary. Clara's life in the Cook home was only mildly better than that of her aunt and young cousin. She was allowed to attend school full time and had piano lessons. Her mother's motivation for both was purely economic. Anne wanted Clara to have an education so she could keep the financial records for her sporting house and bootleg liquor sales. Clara's musical training was put to use at the brothel entertaining clients as they waited for the women to greet them. Mary was allowed to attend school only sporadically, instead focusing on her chores on the farm. If either of the girls failed to do what they were told, they were beaten.

Frank didn't care for Anne's harsh treatment toward the children, but he lacked the will to do anything about it. At least twice during their relationship, he decided to live in the barn for an extended period of time rather than stay in the farmhouse with his wife. The second of the two incidents that drove him out of the house was when Anne accused him of having an affair with her sister. Frank removed all his things from the room he shared with Anne and transferred them to an empty beet shack on the property. Anne promptly moved into a room with her daughter and then rented out the room she and Frank had shared to a boarder. (It wasn't until the last month of his life in 1936 that he again slept under the same roof as his wife. When Frank died of natural causes, Anne's reaction was again to move into a shared room and rent out her and Frank's room.)

In the autumn of 1912, laborers with the Union Pacific Railroad arrived in North Platte to repair and maintain the tracks that ran through the area. When Anne learned how much the local hotel was charging the railroad to house the men, she decided to rent space in her house to the workers. She charged them as much for the use of a cot in the corner and three meals as the hotels in North Platte and Omaha. Any money the railroad workers had left over after paying room and board went toward evening entertainment provided by Anne's ladies. Migrant farm workers employed by the Cooks at harvest time received the same amenities for the same price. Anne's bank account grew quickly.

In 1920, Anne used some of her income to have a new, bigger farmhouse built. When the home was completed, she hosted a party for the local politicians, their associates, and the police. County commissioners and administrators, state representatives, and the sheriff were all in attendance. Four of the most attractive and popular girls from Anne's parlor house in North Platte made sure all the influential guests had a good time. Bottles of whiskey confiscated by law enforcement from bootleggers and brought to the event by the sheriff and his deputies were served. Anne's own liquor made from a still on her property was also available. Given the nature of the social events she hosted and with the monetary contributions she made to local political campaigns, Anne was able to maintain her illegal dealings without interference.

Anne's connection with officials also won her government contracts, including caring for the county's poorest residents. In May 1923, indigent patients at the Lincoln County Hospital, locally known as the Poor House, were transferred to the Cook farm to live. The cost to house the impoverished patients varied. For the healthy poor, the county was charged one dollar a day; those who were sick or had an injury that needed treatment cost one dollar and a quarter per day; and those who were mentally ill or needed around-the-clock care cost a dollar and a half. Those patients who were able to care for themselves were made to work long hours on the farm and were paid nothing for their toil. Anne treated the poor residents living at the farm with the same contempt she did everyone else who lived there.

In an effort to keep the cost of feeding the county's poor low, Anne withheld food from them. When the orphans who lived at the home cried for something to eat, she threatened to beat them with a buggy whip. Community members aware of the abuse at the Cook farm voiced their displeasure to county leaders. Leaders promised that an investigation would be conducted, but nothing ever transpired. Eventually, concerned parties lost interest and dropped the matter entirely.

Then there was the mysterious death of forty-year-old Sarah Martin, an indigent deaf woman who resided at the farm with her five-year-old son, Joe. On September 8, 1925, Sarah's body was discovered alone in the room she shared with her son. Anne told authorities the woman had said she wasn't feeling well and asked to take the morning off and rest. Anne said that Sarah often had headaches and took medicine to make them go away. By late afternoon, when Sarah hadn't come out of her room, Anne went to check on her. According to what Anne told authorities, Sarah had accidentally swallowed a bottle of carbolic acid instead of the headache remedy. The blinds in the room had been pulled and the room was dark. Anne speculated that in the darkness Sarah had picked up the wrong bottle. Sarah lapsed into a coma before her bladder and kidneys ceased to function from the acid.

Ada Kelly, a prominent and benevolent woman in North Platte, thought the timing of Sarah's death was suspicious. Ada noted that two days prior to her death, Sarah had petitioned the county judge to allow her and her son to live and work elsewhere. The judge had granted the request and mother and child were to move to Phelps County, some sixty-five miles away, so Sarah could work as a housekeeper for an elderly couple. Anne was outraged that Sarah was leaving. Not only would she be losing a pair of good workers around the farm but also the county stipend paid to support Sarah and her little boy. Ada and other members of the community wanted Anne arrested for murder, but with no physical evidence or any witnesses linking her to Sarah's death, the police could do nothing. Sarah Martin was buried at the North Platte cemetery for a cost of forty-five dollars, and the care of her son was completely turned over to Anne.

To improve her image and secure a continual contract to care for the county's poor, Anne held a number of prayer meetings in her front yard. She prevailed upon the pastor of the largest church in Hershey to lead these prayer meetings. Clara played the piano before and after the short services, and lemonade and pastries were served. Some of the attendees purchased bootleg whiskey from Anne at the conclusion. Anne's liquor business flourished at the prayer services, and, at the pastor's request, she eagerly agreed to host more events.

Unhappy residents of Anne's poor house attempted to run away during the prayer meetings and other public events held at the Cook farm. Anne was too distracted to keep an eye on all the patients, and, while her attention was divided, they tried to make their escape. The sheriff and his men would always find the patients and bring them back. An elderly man by the name of Pitts, who was the subject of much ridicule by Anne, attempted to escape after only three months living under her roof. His body was found floating in an irrigation ditch not far from the farm. Crip Jenson, another aged gentleman who disapproved of the home, was never found. Jenson had a crippled leg and often complained about being hungry and not being allowed to take a bath. Neighbors suggested the police search the farm for the man's remains. The implication was that Anne had killed Jenson and buried him in her apple orchard. Authorities on Anne's payroll excused every death at the farm as accidental and characterized every missing person case as an investigation in process.

Anne and her daughter Clara frequently spread their money—acquired from the poor house contract, prostitution, and bootlegging—on the kitchen table to be counted. Joe Martin told the author who wrote the biography of Anne Cook that the pair stacked 100 dollar bills in piles and then stuffed them into sacks. "The money bags were sometimes six or seven stacks thick," he remembered. Mother and daughter often fought over the money that accumulated; neither thought the amount was close to what they needed to be independently wealthy.

Prohibition ended in December 1933, and the bootlegging business fell off considerably. Anne was forced to find another way to generate income. In addition to adding a few new women to the house of ill-repute she owned and operated, Anne decided to venture into banking. Irrigation companies that needed funds to upgrade the system statewide issued multiple irrigation warrants, similar to bonds. Using all the political leverage she had, Anne purchased many of those warrants. In doing so she was in effect loaning money to the irrigation companies for the work that had to be done. She imposed a seven percent interest rate on the payback of those funds. The warrants more than made up for the money Anne was no longer getting from bootleg whiskey.

In February 1934, a new county commissioner took office and dared to accept bids from other caregivers to handle the community's poor. He was not intimidated by Anne and had zero tolerance for corrupt politicians. He took away the contract that Anne had managed to monopolize for eleven years. The job then went to a team of individuals who drastically improved the life of the region's impoverished.

Three months after the poor house business was given to another bidder, Anne was still furious over the matter. That anger spilled over into the argument she had with her daughter. Clara's death was the source of much gossip, and few believed Anne's version of the fatal altercation. In private, Anne complained about the rumormongers, but in public she played the part of the grieving mother. The insurance representative who called on the Cooks several weeks after Clara's demise did not suspect any foul play. He was a stranger in the area and hadn't heard anything bad about Anne or the rumors surrounding Clara's death. The sorrow Anne displayed over the loss of her daughter when he handed her an insurance check seemed genuine. The face value of the policy was 10,000 dollars. Anne claimed double indemnity because Clara's death was deemed accidental. She used the money to purchase more land.

And she found new investments. Anne established herself as a bank for men who operated backroom gambling parlors and slot machines. The majority of the meetings Anne had with the bosses of the criminal enterprises she bankrolled were held at her own kitchen table at the farm. It was during

When Anne Cook died in 1952, she was buried with her husband, Frank, and her daughter, Clara, in North Platte Cemetery. Frank and Anne each have a name marker behind the main tombstone. Clara's headstone rests beside the family grave marker.
COURTESY OF VICTOR RAMIREZ

one of those meetings in December 1936 that she was informed of a competitor from Miami who had moved to Lincoln County and was threatening to take control of all the crooked activities in the area. Anne devised a plan to scare the out-of-towner into leaving using her adopted son, Joe. She would force Joe to visit the man; later she would go to the sheriff and report that the man had sodomized the boy. Anne assured her associates that she could make Joe testify to the act in a court of law. The accusation would be recanted if the competitor promised to take his business elsewhere. The threat had the desired outcome, but there was another opponent waiting in the wings to take Anne on, county attorney Sam Diedrich. He was determined to end the long reign of gambling and prostitution in the area.

By early 1941, the criminal element in Lincoln County had all but gone. Anne's associates moved their businesses to Idaho, and she then decided it was time to retire. The sixty-three-year-old woman sold her brothels and slowly dissolved her other criminal ventures. The irrigation warrants she held continued to yield a large amount of money.

Anne Cook died on May 27, 1952, from natural causes. She bequeathed her ill-gotten fortune to friends. She left nothing to her sister Liz, her niece Mary, or her adopted son Joe, all of whom she had abused and worked as slaves. She was laid to rest with her daughter Clara and husband Frank.

CHAPTER TEN

MA BARKER

Most Wanted Mother

I t was a raw, gusty day in mid-January 1934 when Edward Bremer dropped his daughter off at Summit School on Goodrich and Lexington Avenues in St. Paul, Minnesota. Parents and children in heavy overcoats and mufflers hurried across the street and past Edward's car on their way to the building. A light snow began to fall as he pulled away from the elementary school onto Goodrich Avenue toward his office. Edward was the president of the Commercial State Bank and had traveled the same route to work for years.

Each morning he waved goodbye to his little girl at 8:25 A.M. and proceeded on to his job by 8:30 A.M. The Lincoln sedan he drove was comfortable and warm. Music spilled from the radio as he contemplated the paperwork waiting for him on his desk. But this would prove to be no ordinary day. When Edward came to a stop sign on Lexington Avenue, a big-boned man in a blue suit streaked with mud ran to the driver's side window. He was holding a gun.

Edward sat stunned as the armed man flung the door open and shoved the weapon into his side. "Move over," the man barked. Before Edward had a chance to comply, the passenger's side door was jerked open and a tall, athletically built character leaned inside the vehicle. The man struck Edward on the head several times with a blunt instrument. Edward slumped in his seat, and the man with the gun pushed him onto the floor.

Drivers honked at the thugs as they veered around the stopped car. They were unaware of what was taking place—simply annoyed by the disruption to their morning commute. As quickly as he could, the felon on the passenger's side of the sedan shoved a pair of dark goggles on Edward's face and taped them to his head, completely obstructing Edward's vision. A gag was shoved into his mouth and secured in place with a piece of cord. The driver put the car in gear. The thug who knocked Edward unconscious jumped out of the vehicle and hurried to his own car. Both vehicles raced from the scene.

The gunman behind the wheel of Edward's car smiled to himself as he eyed the stupefied victim lying on the front seat floorboard. He removed a newspaper clipping from his suit pocket and tossed it on the seat beside him. A photograph of Edward was front and center. The story under the picture noted that "New Bank President Edward George Bremer is a member of the Bremer family, one of the wealthiest and most prominent families in St. Paul. He is the son of Adolf Bremer, part owner of the Jacob Schmidt Brewing Company, and the nephew of Otto Bremer, Chairman of the American National Bank. Edward Bremer is married and has one daughter."

Fred Barker, a quick-tempered, short man with a dark but dynamic presence, who was completely free of self-doubt, drove the vehicle following the sedan. Fred was the ringleader in the Barker-Karpis gang, one of the most formidable gangs in the 1930s. The gang's twenty-five members routinely stole from banks and jewelry stores, robbed gas stations, and kidnapped and held victims for hefty ransoms. By 1934, the gang had stolen hundreds of thousands of dollars in cash and merchandise and was highly sought after by the FBI.

Fred adjusted his rearview mirror and exchanged a look with Alvin Karpis, another leader of the gang sitting in the back seat of the car. Alvin possessed coal-black hair and a sinister smile that had earned him the nickname "Creepy." Fred nodded approvingly at Alvin. "Ma would be proud," Fred bragged. "No doubt," Alvin agreed. Fred's mother was the infamous Arizona Barker, also known as Kate Barker. She was known to law enforcement as the mastermind of the gang that at one time included all four of her outlaw sons.

Arizona Barker, also known as Kate, or "Ma," Barker. COURTESY OF THE FEDERAL BUREAU OF INVESTIGATION

All the members of the Barker-Karpis gang, blood related or not, affectionately referred to Kate as Ma.

The Barker-Karpis gang hatched the plan to kidnap Edward Bremer in late December 1933. Two men with the organization had spotted Edward at a local bowling alley and recognized him from an article in the *St. Paul Daily* newspaper that told of his profession and wealthy ties. Members of the gang planned to abduct Edward and hold him for ransom. Fred and Arthur, Ma Barker's youngest sons, agreed the ransom would allow their mother to live in style in a roomy log cabin home of her own near a lake where she would never struggle financially. At the time, Ma lived quietly in an apartment on South Shore Drive in Chicago, Illinois, waiting for her boys to finish their illegal business and hurry home to hide out.

On January 17, 1934, a ransom note demanding 200,000 dollars for the release of Edward Bremer was delivered to a close friend of the Bremer family. The note warned the friend from taking the matter to the police, stated the denominations of the bills to be used in the payoff, and told how long he had to gather the ransom. An ad was to be placed in the personal column of the *Minneapolis Tribune* informing the kidnappers that the money was ready to be picked up.

Desperate for help, the Bremer family contacted the authorities. When the Barker-Karpis gang found out the police were involved, they were enraged. Fred and Arthur, also known as Doc, loaded Edward into his Lincoln, beat him severely, transferred him to another vehicle, and abandoned the Lincoln sedan.

The authorities found Bremer's car the following day. Blood was spattered on the steering wheel, seats, gearshift lever, and floor. The police and the Bremer family suspected Edward had been killed. A second ransom note found in the vehicle told them he was still alive. The gang gave the Bremer family one more chance to pay the ransom. They directed the family to follow a series of complicated instructions as a penance for not taking their initial demand seriously. The family complied. Once the money was dropped off and the gang members were sure there would be no further interference from the law, their victim was set free. Edward Bremer was released near the city of Rochester, Minnesota, at 8 P.M. on February 7, 1934, more than three weeks after his capture. And the Barker boys and their accomplices were nearly a quarter of a million dollars richer.

Although Bremer had been blindfolded during the entire twenty plus days he had been held captive, he was able to provide FBI agents with descriptions of specific sounds he heard—construction equipment, jack hammers, big-rig trucks, cement mixers—that ultimately helped lead officers to the location where the kidnappers had held him prisoner. Bureau investigators managed to track purchases made by the felons before and during the ordeal to the F&W Grand Silver Store. An employee identified a photograph of Doc Barker and told authorities she had sold him tape, rope, and goggles. Doc, his brother Fred, Alvin Karpis, and Charles Fitzgerald were wanted for their involvement in numerous crimes, including the kidnapping of six individuals over a three-year period—Edward Bremer being one of them.

FBI director J. Edgar Hoover believed Ma Barker was the brains of the notorious Barker-Karpis gang, calling the shots and directing her outlaw sons and their associates in their criminal enterprises. Ma Barker and her boys were among the first criminals to be named "public enemies." Kidnapping Edward Bremer, whose family were personal friends of President Franklin Roosevelt, earned them the title.

Kate Barker was born Arizona Donnie Clark on October 8, 1873, in Ash Grove, Missouri. At age eighteen, Arizona married George E. Barker, and the couple made their home in Aurora, Missouri. George held down several jobs during the couple's nearly forty-year marriage; he worked for the water company, the railroad, and the mining firms in the area. The Barkers had four sons: Herman, born in 1894, Lloyd in 1896, Arthur in 1899, and Fred in 1903. Her boys affectionately called her Ma.

Shortly after Fred was born, the family moved to Webb City, Missouri. Webb City was a mining community with a saloon on every corner and struggling, hopeful miners in every saloon. George tried to keep his sons away from the questionable elements in the rowdy community. He took the boys fishing, taught them to hunt, made sure they went to school, and assigned chores around the house. Ma disagreed with her husband's child-rearing methods. She thought he was too strict and frequently kept him from disciplining the boys when they did something wrong. Tired of waging war with his wife and battling rebellious sons, George gave in to Ma's methods.

From an early age the Barker boys were involved in numerous petty crimes. Ma insisted the four were simply high-strung and a little mischievous. Business owners they had stolen items from and neighbors whose homes they had broken into thought otherwise. Concerned citizens took their complaints about the boy's behavior to their father. George referred all grievances to Ma. She never failed to champion her sons no matter what they were accused of doing.

If indeed her young boys were guilty of a crime, she was always quick to plead for leniency. As the boys grew older, they became more daring and their misdeeds more serious. By the time eldest son Herman was fifteen, the brothers had participated in gas station robberies and car thefts. The police were constantly at the Barker home questioning the boys about unlawful activities. Ma believed her sons were being persecuted by the authorities, and she insisted George move the family elsewhere. Trouble followed the Barkers to Joplin, Missouri, and soon another move was required. By mid-1910, they had relocated to Tulsa, Oklahoma. Herman was fifteen, Lloyd was thirteen, Doc was eleven, and Fred was seven years old.

For a brief time the police were not regular visitors at the Barker home, though there were limited problems at school. "For the most part," George later observed, "we were like everyone else in our neighborhood, struggling to make ends meet and doing as we should."

But Ma was not content living in their dilapidated one-story house. She wanted more. George worked three jobs to care for his wife and sons, but Ma insisted he do better. And she didn't let his nominal salary keep her from buying expensive clothing and furniture on credit. Arguments arose between the two whenever the bills arrived. Ma refused to curtail her spending and accused George of being a "shiftless individual with no desire to maintain any high plans socially."

Restless and tired of listening to his parents bicker, Herman left home at age nineteen in 1914 and drifted back to Missouri. Between June 1914 and November 1915, Herman was arrested four times. His offenses included beating a woman and armed robbery. After robbing a grocery store with two other men in Webb City, Herman returned to Tulsa to hide out. Police apprehended him there after he burgled a number of homes.

Arthur was the next to be arrested. He stole a car belonging to a federal employee in Muskogee, Oklahoma. More than 300 dollars in cash and stacks of confidential government records were inside the car when it was taken, and, although the vehicle was eventually found, the records were never retrieved. Through a series of blunders on the part of the police, Arthur avoided jail because of a lack of proof. He wasn't as lucky with the second vehicle he stole from the parking lot of a Tulsa grocery store. The nineteen-year-old was convicted of automobile theft in early 1919 and wasn't released until late 1920.

As Arthur was leaving jail, Fred was being escorted in. He, too, had been arrested for stealing a car. Ma stood by her youngest son's side when they appeared before the judge. After promising that Fred would stay out of trouble, the pair left the courthouse together. Two weeks later Fred was arrested for possession of stolen car parts. Again Ma convinced the judge to let her son go free.

Although Lloyd's criminal activities were restricted to vagrancy and picking pockets, the police responded to more than one complaint about him from residents near the Barker home for his misdeeds.

When Ma Barker's boys weren't in jail, they were in the company of a street gang known as the East Side gang. The twenty-member gang, to which all four Barker boys belonged, specialized in burglarizing homes. Between 1922 and 1928, the men had graduated from home invasions and hijacking cars to armed robbery and murder.

After nearly four decades of being a father and husband, George Barker had his fill of his sons' behaviors and the excuses his wife made for them. He wanted out of the marriage and Ma did not object. Her first priority was her sons. Although they were grown, they continued to live at home off and on as they went in and out of prison. Ma cooked and cleaned for them, acted as their confidante and alibi, and interceded on their behalf whenever the police came looking for them. George left his family and the spotlight of the authorities' watchful eye in 1928. He moved to Joplin, Missouri, where he ran a small filling station and served as caretaker of a campground. He lived a quiet life until his death in 1940.

Ma Barker sacrificed in every area of her life for her boys, and she expected the same dedication from them. She doted on the four and encouraged them to challenge anyone who stood in the way of what they wanted to do. She blamed law enforcement for her sons' troubles. "My boys would be all right if the law would let them alone," she repeatedly told the courts.

Young women attracted to the life of an outlaw kept company with Herman, Arthur, Lloyd, and Fred. Ma objected to the way they would monopolize her sons' time and so she made trouble for the women as often as she could. She disclosed conversations she had with the women to the boys and stressed any negative comments made about the way they were being treated. Ma would put the Barker boys in situations where they would have to choose between her or their girlfriends. The criminals never went against their mother.

Ma had a paramour or two of her own after George left. Arthur Dunlop, alias George Anderson, courted Ma, and she convinced George to go into business with her sons shortly after the two moved in together. The Barker boys and their gang were regular guests at George and Ma's place. Ma preferred it that way. She believed if she were around when her sons got into serious trouble, she could keep them from doing long stretches of time in prison. "It didn't always work," fellow gang member Alvin Karpis told reporters at the *Hutchinson News* after he was paroled in 1979. "No amount of begging a judge or jury was going to stop the law from putting them away one by one."

Ma couldn't protect her paramour or her sons from a violent end either. Herman was the first of Ma's sons to go. He died from a self-inflicted gunshot wound in August 1927. Herman had been arrested in early January 1927 for bank robbery. With the help of his wife, Carol, he escaped jail. Herman and his Cherokee Indian bride traversed the West for seven months before traveling back to his home state of Missouri. In need of money to make it to a hideout in Joplin, he decided to team up with a pair of bandits and rob an icehouse in Newton, Kansas. Police tracked the thieves to Wichita, and a gun battle erupted. Surrounded by lawmen, Herman took his own life rather than surrender.

Ma was devastated. Her reaction was to tighten the reigns on the three children she had left. Lloyd, Arthur, and Fred rebelled against her sometimes oppressive grip. Ma wanted to be the sole female voice in her sons' lives. When they were home, she wanted them with her all the time. She wanted to make all their decisions for them, including who they saw socially and what jobs would be best for them.

Between December 16, 1932, and August 30, 1933, the three Barker boys were on parole after having served long periods of time in prison—Lloyd for stealing mail, Fred for bank robbery, and Arthur for murder. While on parole, the Barker brothers and other members of their gang robbed banks in Nebraska and Minnesota, kidnapped two wealthy businessmen, and were involved in the killing of four police officers. Also, in April 1932, George Anderson's body was found dumped in a lake near Webster, Wisconsin. He'd been shot three times; police found a single bloodstained woman's black glove nearby.

Throughout this period, Ma lived in a small house north of the railroad tracks in Tulsa. She took the boys in when they needed to "cool off" after the robberies, and her place became a key location for meeting up with other members of the gang—as well as developing relationships with other gangs. Ma made bond once or twice to free her sons and other gang members so they could "jump bail" and disappear. Law enforcement would have liked to arrest Ma Barker, but they were unable to prove her actual involvement in any of the gang's crimes. Criminals visited her and skipped out of town before officers could arrive; due to the communication system of the underworld, it was virtually impossible to obtain necessary evidence. There was no one and nothing to prove that Ma had harbored fugitives or aided them in any of their crimes.

When she learned of it, Ma Barker was genuinely surprised that her sons Arthur and Fred were involved in kidnapping wealthy banker Edward Bremer. The Justice Department identified Alvin Karpis and Arthur Barker as the leaders of the criminal group behind the abduction of Bremer. Ma proved

Fred and Ma Barker rented this two-story cottage on Lake Weir in Ocklawaha, Florida. FBI agents surrounded the cottage and called for the surrender of the Barkers. The ensuing firefight left both Barkers dead. COURTESY OF THE FEDERAL BUREAU OF INVESTIGATION

The Barkers were heavily armed at the cottage, as evidenced by the cache of weapons recovered by agents after the firefight. COURTESY OF THE FEDERAL BUREAU OF INVESTIGATION

uncooperative when questioned about the incident in February 1934. Unlike some of the women romantically involved with gang members who inadvertently led police to their individual hideouts, Ma was the soul of discretion.

In November 1934, Ma left the Midwest in the dead of the night. Apart from her sons and a friend who managed a hotel on Lake Weir near Ocala, Florida, no one knew her whereabouts. Ma Barker's disappearance did not deter federal authorities from tracking down Arthur and Fred. Law enforcement found Arthur at his girlfriend's apartment in Chicago on January 8, 1935—a year after the crime. Among the items the police confiscated were a machine gun that had been used to kill a police officer in 1933, several rifles, a cache of ammunition, and a map of Ocala, Florida, showing Lake Weir.

Special agents immediately set out for Florida, where they discovered Ma Barker and her son Fred in a cottage on the lake. On January 16, 1935, at 6:30 A.M., officers surrounded the small home and leveled their guns at every door and window. Authorities shouted to the occupants to come out with their hands up. For a few minutes there was no response, then a voice from inside the house called out, "All right. Go ahead." Thinking the comment was an indication that the people in the cottage were going to surrender, the police waited anxiously for the criminals to exit. The front door slowly opened, and the muzzle of a machine gun appeared. Without warning, shots struck the agents standing nearest the home. The authorities answered the gunfire with tear gas bombs, rifle fire, and machine guns. Witnesses at the scene told newspaper reporters later that the "rapid succession of gunfire sounded like a war."

The gunfire finally ceased at 11 A.M., and authorities entered the home. More than 1,500 rounds of ammunition had struck the cottage. Fred's body was found sprawled on the floor with eleven machine gun slugs in his shoulder and three in his head. Ma Barker was lying in a heap by the front door with a machine gun in her hand. A portion of the drum of ammunition in her weapon had been exhausted. She had been hit by only one bullet that pierced her heart. A search of the house uncovered 14,000 dollars in 1,000 dollar bills. It was determined by the serial numbers on the bills that the money was part of the funds obtained for Edward Bremer's ransom. A small arsenal including shotguns and pistols was found, as well as a letter to Fred from Arthur:

Hello, Everyone. How is the old sunshine down there? Fine I hope. Boy it is not so hot up here for we are having some winter. I bet you are not catching no fish now for I think I caught them all when I was down there. I have not seen our other brother yet, but will do so soon enough and see if he won't come down there. Tell Ma I'm fine and that I said hello.

Ma Barker and her son Fred were deserted in death by their partners in crime, and their bodies remained unburied from January 16 until October 1, 1935. On October 1, 1935, Ma and Fred were buried at an unkempt countryside graveyard known as the Williams Timberland Cemetery in Welch, Oklahoma. It was estimated that approximately twenty-five people attended the services, which included six undertakers and a handful of relatives and curious onlookers. The minister invoked the blessings of the Deity upon the surviving members of the family; he qualified the request for such blessings with the statement "If it be Thy will." The pair are buried next to the grave of Herman Barker, Ma's oldest son.

In late 1935, Arthur "Doc" Barker was tried and convicted for his participation in the kidnapping of Edward Bremer. He was sentenced to life in prison and sent to Alcatraz. Four years later, he was fatally shot while trying to escape. He is buried in Coloma, California. Lloyd Barker served more than ten years at Leavenworth Prison for robbing a U.S. Mail facility. After being paroled in 1942, he joined the Army and worked as a cook for a POW camp during World War II. After the war he was employed at a bar and grill in Denver, Colorado. On March 18, 1949, Lloyd was shot and killed by his estranged wife. He is buried in Denver.

According to FBI records, there was no one to blame for the violent end of the Barker boys but Ma Barker herself. Documents claim she "taught her four boys how to rob, kidnap and murder." It also maintains that Ma "gave them private lessons in the fine art of loading and firing a Thompson submachine gun" and that she "patted them on the back when they carried out her carefully planned crimes." As quoted in the *Hutchinson News* on August 29, 1979, gang member Alvin Karpis insisted that Ma Barker was not capable of such things. "She was just a plain little old hillbilly out of the Ozarks," Karpis told reporters. "She never even knew how to use a machine gun."

Ma Barker was sixty-two years old when she was killed. ➤

CHAPTER ELEVEN

PATRICIA CHERRINGTON ᴀɴᴅ OPAL LONG

Sisters in Crime

A n eerie quiet hung in the air as Patricia Cherrington and her companion, Patrick Reilly (who was known simply as Reilly), pulled into the driveway of the Little Bohemia Lodge in Manitowish Waters, Wisconsin, on Sunday evening, April 22, 1934. Patricia slowly got out of the car, pausing to look around for anyone suspicious looking. The thirty-one-year-old woman was dressed in a gray skirt and a jacket that was a bit too tight. Her dark, neatly coiffed hair framed a pleasant but pale face. Bold, generously applied red lipstick accentuated her worried expression. Reilly, a beefy man with sausage-like fingers, stepped out the driver's side of the vehicle and gently closed the door. He drew on the lit cigarette clenched in his teeth and blew the smoke out through his nose. He and Patricia exchanged an apprehensive look.

Dogs barked in the distance. They knew that the yelping animals belonged to the caretaker of the lodge, and their familiar sound seemed to ease the tension. Patricia almost smiled, but the dull pain in her abdomen stopped her. Reilly saw she was hurting and offered to help her into the house.

Suddenly, machine gun fire erupted from every direction. Glass shattered and tires exploded as multiple bullets poured from the nearby woods. Patricia and Reilly dropped to the ground. Muzzle flashes from automatic weapons inside the house lit up the dark trees surrounding the lodge. A barrage of bullets blasted through the maples, and chunks of wood rained down on armed federal agents hiding in the trees. From within the house, John Dillinger, Baby Face Nelson, and several other members of Dillinger's gang shot at the agents rushing the house, hitting one or two before they could make it to the steps of the hideout.

Caught in the crossfire, Reilly jerked open the passenger door and helped Patricia into the seat. Bullets zinged past them, and she screamed when one grazed her face under her right eye. Shell fragments hit her arm and fractured it. As Reilly started the car and threw it into gear, federal agents fired tear gas grenades into the lodge. Dillinger and his men continued shooting. Reilly laid his foot on the gas pedal and turned the wheel of the vehicle. The car spun like a top and sped away from the gun battle, disappearing into the night.

The *El Paso Herald Post* in Texas reported the next day that Patricia and Reilly weren't the only ones who escaped from the resort. Dillinger and his right-hand man, John "Red" Hamilton, both got away. Among the dead were one federal officer and a public works employee who was working in the area when law enforcement officers raided the lodge. Patricia and Reilly quickly made their way to St. Paul, Minnesota, the rendezvous point for Dillinger and his gang members.

Most of Patricia Cherrington's adult life was spent in the company of criminals. She and her sister, Opal Long, craved the excitement of being around desperados. "Men like John Dillinger," she told a parole board in 1935, "were a good piece of company."

Patricia was born in McClure County, Arkansas, on September 26, 1903. Her parents, William and Goldie Long, were farmers. The family relocated to Texas in 1905 and had two other children: Opal "Bernice," born in 1906, and William Jr., born the following year. According to information Patricia shared with a prison social worker in 1935 about her childhood, she enjoyed school and was an excellent student. She graduated the eighth grade at the age of eleven and attended two years of high school. She claimed to have gone on from there to attend the University of Oklahoma and the University of Philadelphia.

By the time she turned fifteen, she had married a man in Tulsa, Oklahoma, and had a baby. Her daughter, Beverly June Young, was born on June 8, 1921. Patricia adored her child but did not like being a wife. She had aspirations of being on stage. An ambitious singer and dancer, she hoped to some day work in New York or Chicago. In 1922, she left her husband and Oklahoma and headed east.

The road to fortune and fame wasn't as easy as Patricia had anticipated. She eventually found employment as a waitress in Chicago. While searching for a job, she had to leave her daughter in the home of a friend. Betty Naetz Minor had a stable home and a young son and was happy to watch Beverly until Patricia was settled. That day would be a long time coming.

The first steady job Patricia found was dancing in chorus lines at various Chicago theatres and speakeasies, taking the stage name Pat Reilly. She earned as much as seventy-five dollars a week; almost half of her wages went to Betty for taking care of her little girl.

Patricia's poor health kept her from going far with her talent. She'd had a difficult time giving birth to Beverly. The procedure the doctors used to deliver the child left her with debilitating scars. In addition to that, her stomach ached continually due to problems with her gallbladder.

In spite of her physical ailments, she was known to many as vivacious and spontaneous. She attracted men who thrived on danger and excitement; she only returned the affections of those who had money and plans to attain more. In December 1931, Patricia met Arthur Cherrington. He was an amiable trumpet player and cab driver who never lacked for cash. Arthur was on parole for armed robbery when he and Patricia were introduced by a mutual friend, Evelyn "Billie" Frechette. (Billie was a struggling actress and the woman who would become John Dillinger's lover and confidante.) Arthur was twenty-eight and had been in trouble with the law off and on from the time he was eleven. He and Patricia shared a common interest in music, art, and poetry. He presented himself to Patricia as an upstanding citizen. He had been trying to earn a living legitimately, but when cab drivers in the city decided to go on strike, he lost his income. Stealing money was his way of solving his debt problems. Patricia didn't object. In January 1932, the couple moved in together.

Between May 31 and June 6, 1932, Arthur and his associates robbed three postal stations in Chicago. Patricia was with Arthur when authorities apprehended the criminals in Michigan City, Indiana, on June 14, 1932. She was sent back to Chicago for questioning and released the following morning. Arthur and his accomplices were indicted and pled guilty to their crimes. Each was sentenced to fifteen years in the U.S. penitentiary. Before Arthur left to serve time at Leavenworth Prison, Patricia accepted a marriage proposal from him, and the couple married.

In order to support herself and her daughter, whom she continued to regularly visit, Patricia returned to the chorus line. After six months of working nearly nonstop, she had a gallbladder attack and was forced to have surgery. Until she could get back on her feet again, she moved in with Arthur's brother and his wife. Patricia wrote her husband often, but she had no intention of being faithful to him. She liked having a man around to visit with and enjoy life. So did her sister Opal. The two spent some time at a speakeasy shortly after Patricia recovered from her operation. It was while they were out enjoying the nightlife that they met John Dillinger for the first time. Both women were impressed with the felon. Patricia would later comment to prison officials that she thought he was "charming" and that "he treated every girl like a lady."

Patricia and Opal decided to share a place at the Marshall Hotel in the spring of 1933. The establishment was a popular meeting spot for members of the underworld. The sisters became friends with a number of men residing at the hotel who worked for Dillinger. Patricia and Opal were well liked. Patricia was outgoing and reckless. Opal was a bit more reserved, but not by much. She was a plump lady with red hair who wore thick eyeglasses. She had a gift for caretaking, and that was the role she assumed when she became romantically involved with Russell Clark, one of Dillinger's henchmen; the two were married not long after. Patricia took up with another of the gang members named Harry Copeland. Their relationship was short lived, however. Harry was arrested and sent to prison in October 1933 for second degree burglary.

In between visits to Copeland at the Indiana State Prison in Michigan City, Indiana, Patricia embarked on a romance with Red Hamilton. Patricia refused to commit to anyone and regarded her daughter as the only true constant in her life. Beverly was never permitted to be around the Dillinger gang. Patricia kept her little girl from even knowing about her association with the outlaws until she was well into her teens. Both Opal and Betty Minor offered to adopt Beverly, but Patricia wouldn't entertain the idea. She deeply loved her child and wanted to keep her.

Although Patricia and Opal did not physically participate in the October 23, 1933, robbery of the Central National Bank of Greencastle, Indiana, they did help hide Dillinger and his men from the police and directly benefitted from the 74,000 dollars stolen. The ladies were compensated for their assistance. It wasn't until after the robbery of the American Bank and Trust Company in Racine, Wisconsin, on November 20, 1933, that authorities began turning their attention to the sisters. One gang member, captured at the scene of the crime, told law enforcement officials about Patricia and Opal, and the pair were then sought for interrogation. Before the authorities could track them down and interview them, both left the area heading in different directions. Opal went to Tucson, Arizona, with Russell Clark, and Patricia traveled to Detroit to look after Red Hamilton; he had been shot in the groin during the holdup of the bank in Indiana. Opal was arrested at the Congress Hotel in Tucson in January 1934. Dillinger, Opal's husband, and two other prominent gang members and their girlfriends, including Dillinger's love interest Billie, were also arrested. All were returned to Chicago. The men were jailed and the women were questioned and then released.

By March 1934, Dillinger had escaped custody from an Indiana jail and was planning to rob the Securities National Bank at Sioux Falls, South Dakota, with Red Hamilton. Red's health had been fully restored by this time thanks in large part to Patricia's care. In the days leading up to the robbery and a few days after the crime took place, Patricia and Opal traveled around the Midwest. They hoped to shake any police that could possibly be following them to their destination, the Dillinger gang's hideout at the Little Bohemia Lodge in Manitowish Waters, Wisconsin.

On March 6, 1934, Dillinger and his men stole 49,500 dollars from the Securities National Bank. On March 13, the desperados robbed a second bank in Sioux Falls, making off with 52,000 dollars. Dillinger and his men converged at the lodge on April 20, 1934. Patricia escaped the FBI raid that occurred on April 22, 1934. Pat Reilly, the man who helped her escape, was

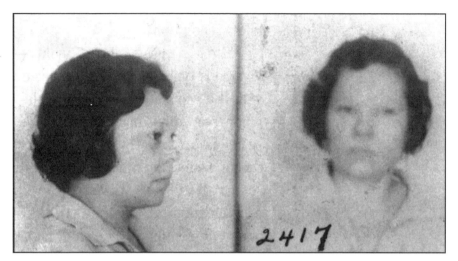

Patricia Cherrington was arrested along with her sister, Opal Long, for her involvement with the John Dillinger gang. She served two years for harboring fugitive John "Red" Hamilton, a lieutenant in Dillinger's gang. COURTESY OF THE FEDERAL BUREAU OF PRISONS

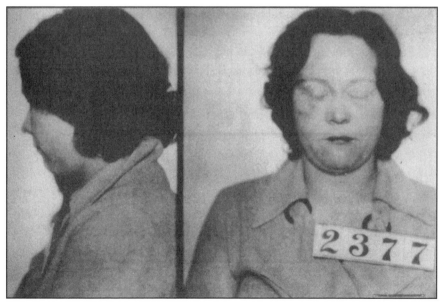

Opal Long served a six-month sentence at the Minneapolis Workhouse after her arrest in 1934. COURTESY OF THE FEDERAL BUREAU OF PRISONS

arrested in June 1934 and sentenced to fourteen months in prison. Patricia's lover Red Hamilton didn't do as well. Dillinger, who shot his way to freedom at Little Bohemia, managed to get word to Patricia informing her that Red was seriously injured. She never saw him again. He died from multiple gunshot wounds, and Dillinger and another associate buried him in a shallow grave.

From April 20 to May 31, 1934, Patricia and Opal tried to keep a low profile. The sisters were in Detroit when Patricia decided she desperately needed to see her daughter. She wanted to give her some money and pay Betty for her care. On their way to visit Beverly, Opal had a car accident. No one was hurt, but the car needed to be repaired before they could continue on. With no money to fix the vehicle, Opal decided to pawn her wedding ring. Fearing the accident and the trip to the pawn shop might have attracted attention from the law, they returned to Detroit. Patricia sent funds to her daughter using a source she thought could be trusted to keep their whereabouts secret. Unbeknownst to the sisters, the source was an informant for the federal government.

On June 1, 1934, Patricia and Opal were tucked inside a room at the Chateau Hotel, waiting, they didn't know for what. Federal agents were told where the sisters were staying, and in the early afternoon the authorities charged into their living quarters and arrested the pair. Both women were placed in solitary confinement at the Bridewell Prison in Cook County, Illinois, to await trial. Patricia was suffering with a hernia at the time of her arrest and was refused medical attention unless she told police everything she knew about Dillinger and his operation. Patricia wouldn't talk. Neither would Opal.

On July 6, 1934, Patricia pled guilty to federal harboring charges. She was sentenced to two years in prison and served her time at the U.S. Detention Farm in Milan, Michigan. Opal Long pled guilty to all charges as well, but, because she displayed remorse over her crimes, she was given a six-month sentence at the Minneapolis Workhouse. Opal missed her niece terribly while she was incarcerated and wrote her several letters. Patricia missed Beverly, too, and in late December 1934, she wrote a Christmas letter to her daughter. The message reflected a sincerely contrite heart and the desire to be a better mother. The editor of the Madison, Wisconsin, newspaper the *Wisconsin State Journal* received a copy of the touching letter and contacted

Patricia through the warden at the prison. He asked her if he could reprint the message. According to the *Wisconsin State Journal* on December 23, 1934, Patricia agreed but added, "Don't crucify the kid by revealing her identity." The letter read:

My Dear Little Girl,

Received your darling letter, dear, and it was mighty precious to me, and my love and happiness attend you wherever you go, and may you never want for friends.

You have already entered your teens, a whole life is ahead of you. You will soon no longer be a child, but a young lady. With young womanhood comes the first real test of what life means. Joys and sorrows will be yours and I want to arm you against the things you will have to endure. The pain of disappointment will come to you many times. Learn to fortify yourself against it by thinking pure and happy thoughts.

Remember that the men and women who accomplish things in this world today are those who laugh in the face of adversity and vow not to be beaten.

Learn to smile at yourself and soon others will smile with you, and happiness will come from the most unexpected sources. Be a carrier of joy, bubble over with happiness, and force your mind to dwell on wholesome things.

Remember, sweetheart that your body is a temple erected by Mother Nature wherein worshippers come to pray, before the shrine of humanity. If you keep your body clean both inside and out, impure worshippers cannot remain long, for the impure things in life come only when our minds and bodies offer no resistance to them.

Remember always that there once lived in Nazareth a Holy Man who showed by his example the possibilities of cleanly living and pure thinking. Read the life of Jesus. View him as a man and emulate his example as far as you are able. He said, 'Do unto others as you would have that they should do unto you.'

I want you to know that a life of service is the happiest one to lead. Serve others joyously and your reward will be great. Carry with you the message of charity and brotherly love. Love everybody. Keep hate out of your soul. It has soured the lips of many who should have been the constant bearers of messages of joy.

Take exercise, breathe good air, bathe often and keep your mind busy.

Fortunately, you are living in the 'age of women,' therefore I may say to you – amount to something. Vow to be more than a parlor ornament, vow to do something that will place your name among the annals of the blessed.

You possess talents far above those possessed by the average little girl, develop them, and let your light shine as a beacon to guide others into the path of action. Dream of good things to come and vow to be ready to receive them when they do come.

Be just, be generous, be kind to those around you, so that when dark days come you will have plenty of friends to help you bear your trouble.

Your mother loves you dearly, and I am ambitious for you, and will help you as far as you will let me. Come to me with whatever you do.

May God bless my little girl, and keep her strong in body, mind and spirit and make you ever ready to take advantage of your divine attributes.

Mother may be away from you for a while and I want to know you will always be the same obedient daughter I have taught you to be. Keep this letter and when in doubt read it over again.

I love you, daughter of mine, always. Your Mother.

Patricia was released from prison in late 1936 and returned to Chicago to work as a waitress. She was rearrested on suspicion of theft on April 21, 1938. According to the *Wisconsin State Journal* on April 22, 1938, "Chicago police seized Mrs. Cherrington at a hotel in the heart of the city. She was in the company of two known thieves and charged with stealing. Mrs. Cherrington said she knew nothing about the crime she was accused of and pleaded for her release." All charges against Patricia were dropped after a full investigation was completed.

Patricia Cherrington, who had struggled with poor health since her gallbladder attack, died on May 1, 1949. The *Logansport* [Indiana] *Press* reported on May 6, 1949, that none who attended Patricia's funeral wanted to reveal their identity. "About fifty determinedly anonymous friends turned up today to pay final respects to a one-time Dillinger gang moll," the article began. "Patricia Cherrington was found dead in her North Clark Street hotel room. A coroner's physician estimated she had died of natural causes five days before." Newspapers reported that after her body had been taken to the county morgue, a sister, Mrs. Opal Long-Kosmal, claimed the body.

"Today's brief services at a near North Side funeral home were read by a minister who left by a side door," a newspaper article read. "Immediately afterward, Mrs. Long-Kosmal told newsmen, 'I don't think the minister cares to have his name revealed.'"

The mourners felt the same way. None of those attending would identify themselves, and the guest register at the funeral home had been removed.

Patricia was buried in an unmarked grave in Wunders Cemetery in Chicago, Illinois. She was forty-five years old when she died.

Reporters for the *Logansport Press* believe Opal gave a false last name when she was interviewed at her sister's funeral. Opal died of heart failure on July 31, 1969, in Chicago. She was sixty-three years old. ⊷

REFERENCES

FLORA MUNDIS
Books

Shirley, Glenn. West of Hell's Fringe: Crime, Criminals & the Federal Peace Officer in the Oklahoma Territory 1889-1907. University of Oklahoma: Norman, Oklahoma, 1990.

Newspapers

Cedar Rapids Evening Gazette, Cedar Rapids, Iowa, September 26, 1893.

_____, December 8, 1893.

El Reno Democrat, El Reno, Oklahoma, August 17, 1894.

Guthrie Daily Leader, Guthrie, Oklahoma, May 11, 1892.

_____, December 17, 1893.

San Antonio Daily Light, San Antonio, Texas, August 16, 1894.

ELIZABETH REED
Books

Kelsheimer, Rick. *The Hanging of Betsey Reed: A Wabash River Tragedy on the Illinois Frontier.* BookSurge Publishing: Lawrence County, Illinois, 2009.

Newspapers

Daily Record, Lawrence, Illinois, February 6, 1962.

Lawrence County News, Lawrenceville, Illinois, August 18, 1932.

Mt. Vernon Register-News, Mount Vernon, Illinois, June 6, 1968.

Journals/Historical Quarterlies

Monroe, B. D. "Life and Services of William Wilson, Chief Justice of the Illinois Supreme Court." *Journal of the Illinois State Historical Society* 11 (October 1918).

Websites

A Grave Interest blog, "Elizabeth Reed: First Woman Executed by Hanging," www.agraveinterest.blogspot.com.

Elliott, Ray. "The Hanging of Elizabeth Reed," www.talespress.com.

Legal Documents

Probate Court of Lawrence County, State of Illinois, In the Matter of the Estate of Elizabeth Reed Deceased.

Last Will and Testament of Mrs. Elizabeth Reed.

People of State of Illinois vs. Elizabeth Reed, Indictment for Murder, Transcript of Justices' Proceeding.

KATE BENDER
Books

Hardy, Allison. *Kate Bender, The Kansas Murderess: The Horrible History of An Arch Killer.* Haldeman-Julius Publications: Girard, Kansas, 1944.

James, John T. *The Benders in Kansas.* Mostly Books: Pittsburg, Kansas, 2004.

Lee, Wayne C. *Deadly Days in Kansas.* Caxton Press: Caldwell, Idaho, 1997.

Newspapers

Chicago Evening Journal, Chicago, Illinois, July 30, 1880.

Milford Mail, Milford, Iowa, June 18, 1901.

New York Times, New York, New York, May 6, 1910.

Warren Ledger, Warren, Pennsylvania, August 13, 1880.

Washington Post, Washington, D.C., June 5, 1911.

Websites

American Hauntings, "The Bloody Benders," www.prairieghosts.com.

FANNIE AND JENNIE FREEMAN
Newspapers

News Palladium, Benton Harbor, Michigan, June 16, 1906.

San Antonio Daily Light, San Antonio, Texas, July 5, 1903.

_____, July 6, 1894.

SARAH QUANTRILL
Books

Leslie, Edward. *The Devil Knows How to Ride: The True Story of William Clarke Quantrill and His Confederate Raiders.* De Capo Press: New York, 1998.

Wright, Mike. *What They Didn't Teach You About the Civil War.* Presidio Press/Random House: New York, 1998.

Newspapers

Daily Milwaukee News, Milwaukee, Wisconsin, May 5, 1864.

Fort Wayne Weekly Gazette, Fort Wayne, Indiana, August 31, 1888.

Kansas City Star, Kansas City, Missouri, May 23, 1926.

Louisville Journal, Louisville, Kentucky, October 11, 1864.

Magazines

Breihan, Carl. "Kate King Quantrill." *Real West Magazine* 20, no. 153 (September 1977).

Journals/Historical Quarterlies

Christopher, Adrienne Tinker. "Kate King Clarke—Quantrill's Forgotten Girl Bride." *Westport Historical Quarterly* 4, no. 1 (June 1968).

Williams, Burton. "Quantrill's Raid on Lawrence." *Kansas Historical Quarterly* 34, no. 2 (Summer 1968).

Websites

Civil War Women blog, "Sarah Quantrill," www.civilwarwomenblog.com.

Millers Paranormal Research, "William Clarke Quantrill," www.millersparanormalresearch.com.

The Handbook of Texas Online, "William Quantrill Clarke," www.tshaonline.org/handbook/online/articles.

Cathy Barton and Dave Para, "Cathy Kate's Song," www.bartonpara.com.

ALICE IVERS

Books

Fielder, Mildred. *Poker Alice.* Centennial Distributors: Deadwood, South Dakota, 1978.

Rezatto, Helen. *Tales of the Black Hills.* Fenwyn Press: Rapid City, South Dakota, 1989.

Newspapers

Morning News, Florence, South Carolina, April 29, 1929.

Websites

A Reference and Travel Guide for the Rocky Mountain States, "Poker Alice Ivers," www.sangres.com.

BELLE BLACK AND JENNIE FREEMAN
Newspapers

Alva Republic, Alva, Oklahoma, November 7, 1894.

Fort Wayne Sentinel, Fort Wayne, Indiana, May 30, 1896.

Guthrie Daily Leader, Guthrie, Oklahoma, August 14, 1963.

Hutchinson News, Hutchinson, Kansas, August 14, 1895.

Kingfisher Free Press, Kingfisher, Oklahoma, June 27, 1895.

Wichita Eagle, Wichita, Kansas, November 7, 1895.

VICTORIA WOODHULL
Books

Gabriel, Mary. *Notorious Victoria: The Life of Victoria Woodhull, Uncensored*. Algonquin Books of Chapel Hill: Chapel Hill, North Carolina, 1998.

Stowe, Harriet Beecher. *My Wife and I*. Houghton, Mifflin & Company: New York, New York, 1899.

Tilton, Theodore. *Victoria Woodhull*. Golden Age Books: New York, New York, 1871.

Journals/Historical Quarterlies

Horowitz, Helen L. "Victoria Woodhull, Anthony Comstock, and Conflict over Sex in the United States in the 1870s." *The Journal of American History* (September 2000).

Newspapers

Anglo-American Times, London, England, September 30, 1871.

_____, November 23, 1872.

Daily News-Miner, Fairbanks, Alaska, June 11, 1927.

Monticello Express, Monticello, Iowa, November 7, 1872.

New York Times, New York, New York, November 23, 1871.

Oakland Tribune, Oakland, California, March 9, 1964.

Magazines

Harper's Weekly, New York, New York, February 17, 1871.

Websites

Woodhull & Claflin's Weekly Archives, www.victoria-woodhull.com.

ANNE COOK

Books

Yost, Nellie Snyder. *Evil Obsession: The Annie Cook Story*. Tom and Janice Yost Publishing, 1991.

Newspapers

North Platte Bulletin, North Platte, Nebraska, May 30, 1934.

Websites

McCook Daily Gazette, "Annie Cook and Her Evil Obsession," www.mccookgazette.com.

MA BARKER

Books

Winter, Robert. *Mean Men: The Sons of Ma Barker*. Rutledge Books: Danbury, Connecticut, 2000.

Newspapers

Hutchinson News, Hutchinson, Kansas, August 29, 1979.

Legal Documents

Federal Bureau of Investigation File, Barker-Karpis Gang Summary.

Federal Bureau of Investigation File, Bremer Kidnapping, Parts 144 and 459.

PATRICIA CHERRINGTON AND OPAL LONG

Books

Poulsen, Ellen. *Don't Call Us Molls: Women of the John Dillinger Gang*. Clinton Cook Publishing Corp.: Little Neck, New York, 2002.

Newspapers

El Paso Herald Post, El Paso, Texas, April 23, 1934.

Logansport Press, Logansport, Indiana, May 6, 1949.

Wisconsin State Journal, Madison, Wisconsin, December 23, 1934.

_____, April 22, 1938.

_____, August 16, 1938.

Websites

Abbie's Attic, "Arthur Cherrington" and "Patricia Young Cherrington," www.labbiesattic.com.

The Little Bohemia Lodge, "Little Bohemia Lodge History," www.littlebohemialodge.com.

GENERAL REFERENCES
Newspapers

Advocate, Newark, New Jersey, August 4, 1966.

Bismarck Tribune, Bismarck, North Dakota, February 28, 1930.

Evening Independent, Massillon, Ohio, February 20, 1929.

Helena Independent, Helena, Montana, March 30, 1935.

Indiana Evening Gazette, Indiana, Pennsylvania, July 5, 1966.

Lock Haven Express, Lockhaven, Pennsylvania, February 15, 1985.

Logansport Press, Logansport, Indiana, March 23, 1934.

New York Herald, New York, New York, November 3, 1872.

New York Times, New York, New York, December 8, 1887.

_____, November 28, 1968.

Progress, Clearfield, Pennsylvania, December 3, 1948.

Salina Journal, Salina, Kansas, August 7, 2005.

Syracuse Herald, Syracuse, New York, April 16, 1920.

Titusville Herald, Titusville, Pennsylvania, January 17, 1935.

Washington Post, Washington, D.C., June 21, 1908.

_____, June 5, 1917.

World, New York, New York, September 2, 1894.

INDEX

Karpis, Alvin "Creepy" 90, 92, 95, 96, 99

Kelly, Ada 85

King, Malinda 41

King, Robert 41

King, Tom. See Mundis, Flora

King Solomon's Mine, Colorado 51

Knox, Joe 82–83

Knox, Mary 82, 83

L

Labette County, Kansas 18, 20, 30

Lafayette County, Missouri 44

Lawrence, Kansas 39, 41, 45–46

Lawrence County, Illinois 11

Lawrenceville, Illinois 10, 14, 16

Lawson, Eugene 35–37

Leadville, Colorado 50

Lewis, D. C. 9

Lewis, Ernest 5, 7

Lincoln, Abraham 15

Lincoln County Hospital 84

Lincoln County, Nebraska 79–88

Linder, Usher 14

Logan County, Oklahoma 60

Logan, James 12–13, 15

Logansport, Indiana 12

Long, Goldie 101

Long, Opal "Bernice" 103–109
    arrest 105
    and Dillinger gang 101–102

Long, William 101

Long, William Jr. 101

Long-Kosmal, Mrs. Opal. See Long, Opal "Bernice"

Longmont, Colorado 30

Louisville, Kentucky 38, 39, 46

M

McCall, Jack 51

McCleary, H. S. 1–2

McClure County, Arkansas 101

McPherson, Frances. See Bender, Katherine

Madison, Wisconsin 106

Madsen, Chris 5, 7–8

Major County, Oklahoma 58

Manhattan, Colorado 30

Manhattan, New York 33, 63–64

Manhattan Elevated Railroad 33

Manitowish Waters, Wisconsin 100, 104

Martin, Joe 81, 84, 85, 86

Martin, John Biddulph 78

Martin, Sarah 84–85

Matthews, J. (Lincoln County, Nebraska, coroner) 80

Michelson, Herb 69

Michigan City, Indiana 103

Milan, Michigan 106

Milford, Iowa 30

Millerites 16

Minor, Betty Naetz 102, 104

Mount Gilead, Ohio 66

Mundis, Flora 1–9
    arrests 1–2, 5, 7
    as Tom King 1–2, 5–9
    as prostitute 3–4
    and train robbery 5, 7

Mundis, Ora 3

Mundy, Sue. See Clark, Marcellus Jerome

Muskogee, Oklahoma 94

ABOUT THE AUTHOR

Chris Enss has been writing about women of the Old West for more than a dozen years. She loves Western culture and travels extensively, collecting research for her books. She received the Spirit of the West Alive award, cosponsored by the *Wild West Gazette*, celebrating her efforts to keep the spirit of the Old West alive for future generations. She currently lives in a historic gold-mining town in Northern California.